CRANKS

Savouries & Sauces

Compiled by Daphne Swann

Cranks is indebted to Jane Suthering, the well-known home economist. She has worked with Cranks on all its recipe books and has adapted, devised and tested the recipes in this latest series.

Pottery for photography kindly loaned by Craftsmen Potters Shop, Marshall Street, London W1.

© Text Cranks Ltd 1988
© The Work Guinness Publishing Ltd 1988
Editor Beatrice Frei
Art editor David Roberts
Illustrations Suzanne Alexander, Edward Bawden and Jane Lydbury
Cover Ashley Lloyd
Photographs Grant Symon
Published in Great Britain by Guinness Publishing Ltd,
33 London Road, Enfield, Middlesex, England.

Savouries & sauces
1. Vegetarian cookery
I. Cranks Limited
641.5'636   TX837

ISBN 0–85112–390–2

Typeset by Ace Filmsetting Ltd, Frome, Somerset
Printed and bound in Spain by Graficas Reunidas S.A., Madrid

INTRODUCTION

When Cranks opened its first restaurant 27 years ago (in Carnaby Street in London's Soho) its name exactly reflected how most people viewed wholefood and vegetarian restaurants – nutty in more senses than one! Now, of course, the lonely furrow that Cranks then ploughed has become the broad highway for a great many.

From the very beginning Cranks became something of a cult and throughout has remained the benchmark by which all other similar enterprises have to be judged. Not only has there been an unswerving commitment to wholefood and vegetarian food without additives and preservatives (to this day Cranks still use flour from Pimhill Farm in Shropshire, which was one of the first to become totally organic) but there has also been a vigorous experimentation, innovation and creation of new dishes. And although now the food served at any of Cranks' expanding family of restaurants is sophisticated by comparison with the relatively simple fare of the earliest days, there still remains a satisfying practicality and unfussiness in the recipes which is a refreshing change from the pretentiousness of many restaurants and cookbooks.

The continual creation of new dishes has, over the years, produced a vast number of tried and tested recipes – and it's from this repertoire of new dishes that the very best have been selected for inclusion in this series of books.

NOTES ON INGREDIENTS

Agar The vegetarian substitute for gelatine. It is derived from a sea vegetable and produces a slightly cloudy jelly when set. It is available as a powder or in flakes.

Apple concentrate This syrupy brown concentrate is available in bottles from most health food shops.

Arrowroot Used as a thickening agent, this white powder extracted from the rhizome of a herbaceous plant from the West Indies is believed to be helpful in digestive disorders.

Buckwheat The seeds of a plant known as Saracen corn, buckwheat is rich in protein, minerals and the B complex vitamins. Also available ready roasted.

Butter Cranks recommends using an unsalted butter. If preferred, a vegetarian margarine may be substituted in all recipes where butter is stated.

Cheese A wide variety of vegetable rennet cheeses is now being produced. At present, there at least 50 varieties – most health food shops and some supermarkets will offer a good choice. For further information, contact the London Cheese Company, Unit 9, Cedar Way, Camley Street, London NW1.

Coconut Can be bought in various forms – desiccated or shredded (which is finely grated and dried) or creamed. The latter is sold in bars or tubs and can be broken off and melted for use in cooking. Coconut milk powder is sold like dried milk. All can be found in good health food stores or oriental shops.

Couscous A semolina made from hardwheat moistened and rolled in flour. It is used extensively in the Middle East as a grain to accompany spicy stews. Sold ready to cook in health food shops. Follow directions on the packet.

Eggs Cranks uses only free-range eggs in its bakeries, and therefore recommends their use in all the recipes. Many free-range eggs are not graded, but as a guideline, we would use size 3. Always look out for the label 'free range' when buying.

Flours
Cranks uses 100% wholemeal stoneground and organically grown flour in all recipes – thus using the wholewheat berry. White flour has all the valuable bran and germ removed.
Brown rice flour is milled from unpolished rice and can be ground to produce fine, medium or coarse flour. May be used as a thickening agent.
Buckwheat flour produces a fine, dark, speckled flour and is particularly good used in batters.
Cornmeal is a pale yellow flour produced from maize kernels. Used as a thickening agent or in breads and puddings.

Freezing Recipes which are suitable for freezing will be marked by asterisks ***.

Ginger Root ginger should be peeled and then grated.

Herbs Wherever possible, use fresh herbs. If using dried ones, remember the flavour is often more concentrated, so use about half the quantity specified.

Kidney beans All kidney beans must be fast-boiled for a minimum of 15 minutes to destroy a poisonous substance they contain. They should never be sprouted for eating raw.

Nutter A pure white vegetable fat made from nut oils – the vegetarian alternative to lard. Sold in cartons in health food shops.

Oil Sunflower, safflower and soya oil are all good to use in cooking, being mild in flavour and low in saturated fats.

Rice Rice is similar in structure to wheat. It is milled to remove the inedible outer husk, leaving a brownish grain which is the bran-covered rice. This bran is removed to give a white rice. Brown rice, sometimes called natural rice, retains all the valuable minerals and vitamins and is a good source of starch. Its protein content is lower than other grains. It is now possible to get a variety of different brown rice grains, such as short grain, risotto rice, long grain and basmati.

Suet Various vegetable suets are now readily available, made from vegetable oils, with riceflour or wheatflour.

Tahini A thick oily paste made from roasted sesame seeds. Rich in fat, protein and minerals. May be thinned down with water.

Tofu A soya bean curd with a soft delicate texture and pale in colour. Sold in slabs or slices, available plain, with herbs, smoked or marinated. It should be kept refrigerated.

Vegetables
Vegetables should be thoroughly washed. In most cases, the valuable vitamins and minerals are stored in or just below the skin, so it is important not to peel vegetables unless the skin is particularly tough or scarred. Wherever possible, they should be steamed and the vegetable water, which contains valuable juices, should be kept for stock.

Aubergines These dark purple, white or purple mottled pear-shaped vegetables can be bitter when cooked. To avoid this, slice or dice and sprinkle with salt. Leave for 30 minutes to extract the bitter juices. Rinse well and dry thoroughly.

Baby globe artichoke These tiny artichokes may be eaten whole as the hairy choke at the centre of the heart has not yet formed. If necessary, the first outer layer of leaves may be discarded before cooking.

Celeriac A large round knobbly root, closely related to celery with a similar flavour. It may be eaten raw or cooked.

Fennel This large bulbous root, pale green in colour with stalks and herb fronds at the top, is often known as florence fennel. It has a delicate flavour, similar to aniseed, and may be eaten raw or cooked.

Kohlrabi An unusual, hard, turnip-shaped vegetable from the cabbage family. Boiled, steamed or baked, it may be served mashed, puréed or used in stews and casseroles.

Mediterranean tomatoes Large irregular tomatoes weighing about 8 oz (225 g) each. Sometimes known as 'beef' tomatoes because of their firm texture.

Mushrooms These should be wiped only and their stalks scraped clean with a sharp knife. As well as the common mushroom in button, flat or cap shapes, there are now a great variety of cultivated mushrooms, such as *Shiitake*, *Oyster* and *Chestnut*. Also wild mushrooms, like *Chanterelles*, *Ceps*, *Girolles* and *Morels* are now appearing in the shops.

Okra These five- or six-sided, pointed green pods are sometimes known as *Ladies' fingers*. Best eaten cooked and preferably sautéd, as blanching or stewing tends to make them very glutinous.

White courgettes These baby marrows are very pale in colour and much smaller than their more usual green counterparts.

WHOLEMEAL PASTRY CHART
easy guide to quantities

100% wholemeal flour	baking powder	½ butter ½ Nutter	water (approx)
4 oz (100 g)	1 tsp (5 ml)	2 oz (50 g)	4 tsp (20 ml)
5 oz (150 g)	1½ tsp (7.5 ml)	2½ oz (75 g)	2 tbsp (30 ml)
6 oz (175 g)	1½ tsp (7.5 ml)	3 oz (85 g)	2 tbsp (30 ml)
7 oz (200 g)	2 tsp (10 ml)	3½ oz (100 g)	3 tbsp (45 ml)
9 oz (250 g)	2½ tsp (12.5 ml)	4½ oz (125 g)	4 tbsp (60 ml)
10 oz (300 g)	3 tsp (15 ml)	5 oz (150 g)	4 tbsp (60 ml)
12 oz (350 g)	3 tsp (15 ml)	6 oz (175 g)	5 tbsp (75 ml)
14 oz (400 g)	4 tsp (20 ml)	7 oz (200 g)	5 tbsp (75 ml)

Put the flour and baking powder into a basin. Rub in the fat until the mixture resembles fine crumbs. Add sufficient warm water to give a soft but manageable dough. Cover with cling film and leave at room temperature until ready to use.

HOT WATER CRUST PASTRY

Wholemeal flour	1 lb	450 g
Salt	2 tsp	10 ml
Nutter	4 oz	100 g
Milk or milk and water	¼ pt + 4 tbsp	210 ml

Mix the flour and salt. Melt the nutter in the liquid then bring to the boil and add to the flour. Beat with a wooden spoon to form a soft dough.

When cool enough to handle, knead until smooth. Cover with a damp tea towel and leave to rest for 20–30 minutes.

SAVOURIES & SAUCES

In the dictionary, a savoury is described as a relish or an appetizing small dish, but nowadays, with the less formal and enlightened way of eating, a savoury can be far more versatile. Gone are the days of the regular traditional Sunday roast or the 'meat and two veg.' syndrome! With the popularity of wholefood vegetarian eating, the scope of exciting new dishes to prepare is endless – and the savoury plays an important role as the focal point of a meal.

In this book we have introduced a whole new collection of recipes, mostly designed to provide sustaining main dishes. There is a section on sauces and we have recommended their use with particular recipes such as the Mixed grain and walnut pudding with Spinach sauce or the Green and white terrine served with an Almond sauce. However, some of the other sauces would go equally well.

All the recipes are protein rich and follow the traditional wholefood principles which are Cranks' philosophy – many of them may be prepared in advance and freeze well. The recipes which are suitable for freezing are marked by asterisks ***.

There are fibre-rich recipes using beans, pulses and grains like Wheatberry nut and broccoli ragout or the Haricot bean and vegetable pie. A particularly delicious dish is the Layered Mediterranean vegetable pudding using vegetarian suet and made in the traditional style, or the stunning Festive cranberry terrine which would be a winner for any Christmas or celebration cold table.

There are roasts, quiches, pastas, casseroles, soufflés, pancakes, crumbles and pies, and even a new idea for Sunflower sausages to delight a children's party.

BEANSPROUT & TOFU LATKES

Serve these with spicy tomato sauce (see p. 91).

(see p. 91)

Potatoes 1 lb (450 g)
Leek 1
Beansprouts 8 oz (225 g)
Tofu 8 oz (225 g)
Salt & pepper to taste
Oil for frying

Grate the potatoes and finely shred the leek. Place on a clean tea-towel and squeeze out the excess liquid. Transfer to a bowl and add the beansprouts.

Finely chop or crumble the tofu and add to the vegetables. Season generously.

Heat about one tablespoon (15 ml) oil in a large, heavy-based frying pan. Take about one twelfth of the mixture and press it onto the base of the pan to form a small fritter. Make two or three more fritters (depending on the size of the pan) in the same way. Cook over a medium heat for 3 minutes. Turn and press down. Cook for a further 3 minutes or until golden brown on both sides. Remove from the pan and keep warm. Repeat this process until all the mixture is used up.

Serves 4: Makes 12

MACARONI & NUT CURRY

Wholewheat macaroni 10 oz (300 g)
Assorted nuts, such as: almonds, peanuts, walnuts and
hazelnuts, toasted 6 oz (175 g)
Curry sauce (see p. 84) 1 quantity
Salt & pepper to taste

Cook the macaroni in boiling water for about 12
minutes (or according to packet directions). Drain
well. Add the nuts and curry sauce, and reheat gently.
Season to taste.

Variation
Transfer the mixture to a heatproof serving dish and
sprinkle with a generous layer of grated Cheddar
cheese. Place under a hot grill until the cheese is
bubbling.

Serves 4

FELAFEL BURGERS

Chick peas, soaked overnight 3 oz (75 g)
Beaten egg 1 tbsp (15 ml)
Turmeric ¼ tsp (1.25 ml)
Fresh coriander, chopped 1 tbsp (15 ml)
Ground cumin ½ tsp (2.5 ml)
Chilli powder, a pinch
Garlic clove, crushed 1
Tahini paste 2 tsp (10 ml)
Fresh wholemeal breadcrumbs 2 oz (50 g)
Lemon juice 1 tbsp (15 ml)
Salt and pepper to taste
Wholemeal flour to dust
Oil for frying

Drain the chick peas and bring to the boil in fresh water. Reduce the heat, cover and simmer for 45 minutes to 1 hour until tender.

Alternatively, cook in a pressure cooker at 15 lb (7 kg) pressure for 15 minutes. Leave to cool.

Drain the chick peas, reserving 3 tbsp (45 ml) of the cooking water. Place in a liquidizer or food processor with all the remaining ingredients except the flour and oil, and work to a rough paste. Season generously with salt and pepper.

Using floured hands, shape the mixture into 8 'burgers'. Fry in hot oil for 5–6 minutes until golden brown on both sides. Drain on absorbent paper.

Serve warm with natural yoghourt and a salad garnish.

Serves 4: Makes 8
***

GARDENER'S PIE

Oil 2 tbsp (30 ml)
Onion, grated 8 oz (225 g)
Carrot, grated 8 oz (225 g)
Mushrooms, finely chopped 4 oz (100 g)
Brown or green lentils, soaked overnight 4 oz (100 g)
Walnuts, chopped 4 oz (100 g)
Vegetable stock 1 pint (600 ml)
Fresh thyme, chopped 1 tbsp (15 ml)
Tomato purée 2 tbsp (30 ml)
Salt & pepper to taste

TOPPING
Potatoes 2 lb (900 g)
Milk 4 tbsp (60 ml)
Butter 1 oz (25 g)

Heat the oil and sauté the vegetables until tender. Drain the lentils and add to the pan with the walnuts, stock, thyme and tomato purée. Bring to the boil, reduce heat and simmer for 20–25 minutes until tender. Season to taste.

Steam or cook the potatoes in boiling water for 20 minutes until tender. Drain and mash with the milk and butter. Season to taste.

Transfer the vegetable mixture to an ovenproof serving dish and top with the potatoes, spreading the mixture evenly. Either brown under a hot grill or bake at 400°F/200°C/gas mark 6 for 20–30 minutes.

Serves 4
***

LAYERED MEDITERRANEAN
VEGETABLE PUDDING

Butter 1 oz (25 g), Oil 2 tbsp (30 ml)
Aubergine, thinly sliced 8 oz (225 g)
Fennel, thinly sliced 12 oz (350 g)
Red pepper, deseeded and diced 1
Leek, sliced 8 oz (225 g)
Garlic cloves, crushed 2
Strong Cheddar, Stilton or Leicester, grated 6 oz (175 g)
Salt & pepper to taste
Pastry: Wholemeal flour 6 oz (175 g)
Vegetable suet 3 oz (75 g) (see p. 6)
Dried basil 1 tsp (5 ml)
Mustard powder 1 tsp (5 ml)

Place the butter and oil in a large frying pan and sauté the aubergine and fennel for 2–3 minutes. Add the red pepper, leek and garlic and sauté for a further 2–3 minutes. Season generously. Leave to cool.

Mix the ingredients for the pastry together with salt and pepper and mix to a firm dough with about 8 tbsp (120 ml) cold water. Divide into 3 portions.

Butter a 2½ pt (1.5 l) pudding basin and place a lining of greaseproof paper on the base. Roll out one portion of pastry to just fit the base, then roll out the remaining two portions in rounds of graduating size to fit a layer in the centre and at the top of the pudding basin. Place the small circle of pastry in the basin, spoon over half the vegetable mixture and sprinkle with half the cheese. Repeat the layering once more and finish with the last circle of pastry, pressing down gently each time. Cover with buttered greaseproof paper. Secure well. Steam for 2 hours. Unmould onto a serving plate. Serve in wedges.

Serves 4

CRUSTED BAKED BEANS

Haricot beans, soaked overnight 12 oz (350 g)
Onion, chopped 8 oz (225 g)
Carrots sliced 8 oz (225 g)
Black treacle 4 tbsp (60 ml)
Tomato purée 2 tbsp (30 ml)
Mustard powder 1 tbsp (15 ml)
Cloves 4
Salt 1 tsp (5 ml)
Ground pepper ½ tsp (2.5 ml)
Vegetable stock 2 pt (1.2 l)
Butter 2 oz (50 g)
Fresh wholemeal breadcrumbs 3 oz (75 g)
Cheddar cheese, grated 2 oz (50 g)
Parmesan cheese, grated 1 oz (25 g)
Parsley, chopped 4 tbsp (60 ml)

Drain the beans, then place in a flameproof casserole with the next 10 ingredients. Mix well and bring to the boil. Boil for 15 minutes, covered, then transfer to the oven and cook at 300°F/150°C/gas mark 2 for 4 hours, stirring occasionally, until tender.

Combine the remaining ingredients, press onto the surface of the beans and place under a hot grill to brown. Alternatively, increase the oven temperature to 400°F/200°C/gas mark 6 and cook, uncovered, for a further 20–30 minutes until golden brown.

Serves 4–6
***

WHEATBERRY, NUT & BROCCOLI RAGOUT

An exciting combination of flavours makes up this wholesome dish.

Wheatberries, soaked overnight 8 oz (225 g)
Butter 1 oz (25 g)
Onion, chopped 1
Vegetable stock ¾ pt (450 ml)
Broccoli 8 oz (225 g)
Milk ¼–½ pt (150–300 ml)
Raisins 2 oz (50 g)
Creamed coconut 2 oz (50 g)
Whole peanuts, toasted 1oz (25 g)
Whole almonds, toasted 1 oz (25 g)
Lemon, juice of ½
Salt & pepper to taste

Drain the wheatberries and rinse well. Melt the butter and sauté the onion until transparent. Add the wheatberries and stock. Bring to the boil, reduce heat, cover and simmer for 40 minutes.

Meanwhile, cut the broccoli into florets and the stalk into 2.5 cm (1 inch) pieces. Add to the wheatberries with ¼ pt (150 ml) milk, raisins and creamed coconut. Simmer for a further 15 minutes. Stir in the whole nuts, lemon juice, extra milk if necessary and season to taste.

Serves 4

CHILLI BEANPOT

This hot, spicy dish is best made a day in advance to
allow the flavours to mellow.

Kidney beans, soaked overnight 8 oz (225 g)
Oil 2 tbsp (30 ml)
Onions, sliced 2
Garlic cloves, sliced 3
Celery sticks, sliced 4
Green pepper, deseeded and sliced 1
Ground coriander 2 tbsp (30 ml)
Ground cumin 1 tbsp (15 ml)
Tomatoes, chopped 1 lb (450 g)
Tomato purée 4 tbsp (60 ml)
Dried oregano 2 tsp (10 ml)
Dried chillies, crumbled 2–4
Vegetable stock 1 pt (600 ml)
Salt to taste

Drain the kidney beans. Heat the oil and sauté the
onion, garlic, celery, green pepper, coriander and
cumin until the onion is transparent. Add the
remaining ingredients and bring to the boil.

Boil, covered, for 15 minutes, then reduce the heat
and simmer for 1¼ hours until the beans are tender.

Serves 4
***

MUSHROOM & POTATO CURRY

Oil 2 tbsp (30 ml)
Butter 1 oz (25g)
Onions, chopped 2
Root ginger, grated 1 in (2.5 cm)
Cumin seeds 1 tsp (5 ml)
Ground coriander 1 tsp (5 ml)
Turmeric 1 tsp (5 ml)
Chilli powder ¼ tsp (1.25 ml)
Tiny button mushrooms 1 lb (450 g)
Potatoes, diced 1 lb (450 g)
Tomatoes, diced 8 oz (225 g)
Lemon juice 1 tbsp (15 ml)
Vegetable stock ½ pt (300 ml)
Fresh coriander, chopped 2 tbsp (30 ml)
Garam masala 1 tsp (5 ml)
Salt & pepper to taste

Heat the oil and butter and sauté the onions with the
ginger and spices until the onion is transparent. Add
the mushrooms and toss well. Add the potato, tomato,
lemon juice and stock.

Bring to the boil, reduce the heat, cover and simmer
for 30 minutes until tender. Stir in the fresh coriander
and garam masala.

Season to taste.

Serves 4
***

18

MACARONI CHEESEBURGERS

Wholewheat macaroni 4 oz (100 g)
Butter 2 oz (50 g)
Small onion, finely chopped 1
Wholemeal flour 3 oz (75 g)
Mustard powder 1 tsp (5 ml)
Milk ½ pt (300 ml)
Cider or wine vinegar 1 tsp (5 ml)
Cheddar cheese, grated 4 oz (100 g)
Shelled peas, cooked 4 oz (100 g)
Salt & pepper to taste
Free-range eggs, beaten 2
Fresh wholemeal breadcrumbs 3–4 oz (75–100 g)
Oil for frying

Cook the macaroni according to packet directions. Drain well.

Melt the butter and sauté the onion until transparent. Add 2 oz (50 g) flour and the mustard powder. Cook, stirring for 1–2 minutes. Stir in the milk and cook until thickened. Add the vinegar, cheese, peas and macaroni and season to taste. Leave to go cold.

Shape the mixture into 8 'burgers', using the remaining flour. Dip them in the beaten egg and finally in the breadcrumbs. Reshape as necessary.

Heat the oil and fry the cheeseburgers until crisp and golden on both sides – about 5–6 minutes. Drain on absorbent paper.

Serves 4: Makes 8
***

SWEDE & POTATO SOUFFLÉ PUDDING

Any root vegetable may be substituted for the swede.

Swede, roughly chopped 1 lb (450 g)
Potato, roughly chopped 6 oz (175 g)
Butter 1 oz (25 g)
Onion, finely chopped 1
Cheddar cheese, grated 4 oz (100 g)
Milk ¼ pt (150 ml)
Free-range eggs, separated 2
Ground nutmeg ¼ tsp (1.25 ml)
Parsley, chopped 2 tbsp (30 ml)
Salt & pepper to taste

Cook the swede and potato in boiling water until just tender – about 20 minutes. Drain well and mash.

Melt the butter and sauté the onion until transparent. Mix together the swede and potato, onion, cheese, milk, egg yolks, nutmeg and parsley. Season generously.

Whisk the egg whites until stiff and fold into the vegetable mixture. Transfer to a buttered ovenproof dish and bake at 400°F/200°C/gas mark 6 for about 50 minutes until golden brown and just firm to the touch.

Serves 4

COUNTRY VEGETABLES IN CHEESE SAUCE

A simple supper dish.

Swede or celeriac 12 oz (350 g)
Baby carrots 8 oz (225 g)
Leeks 4
Broccoli 8 oz (225 g)
Vegetable stock 1 pt (600 ml)
Single cream ¼ pt (150 ml)
Butter 2 oz (50 g)
Wholemeal flour 2 oz (50 g)
Mustard powder 1 tsp (5 ml)
Cheddar cheese, grated 6 oz (175 g)
Salt & pepper to taste

Cut the swede into small slices about 5 mm (¼ inch) wide. Top and tail the carrots (if large, halve or slice). Cut the leeks into 2.5 cm (1 inch) lengths. Cut the broccoli into florets and the stalks into 2.5 cm (1 inch) lengths.

Place the swede into a large saucepan with the stock. Bring slowly to the boil, cover and simmer for 5 minutes. Add the carrots and cook for a further 10 minutes. Add the leeks and broccoli and cook for 5 minutes more. Drain well, reserving the stock. Make it up to 1 pint (600 ml) with the cream and add a little water if necessary.

Melt the butter and stir in the flour and mustard powder. Cook for 2–3 minutes, stirring. Add the stock and cream. Bring to the boil, stirring, then reduce the heat. Stir in the cheese until it melts, then add the vegetables and warm through gently. Season to taste.

Serves 4
***

FENNEL CASSEROLE

Serve this tasty casserole with risotto rice or mashed potatoes.

Oil 2 tbsp (30 ml)
Onion, sliced 1
Garlic cloves, sliced 2
Fennel bulbs, sliced 1½ lb (675 g)
Sprig of rosemary 1
Sprigs of thyme 2
Chopped tomatoes 14 oz can (400 g can)
Vegetable stock ¼ pt (150 ml)
Salt & pepper to taste

Heat the oil and sauté the onion and garlic until transparent. Add the fennel and sauté for 5 minutes. Add the remaining ingredients, bring to the boil.

Reduce heat, cover and simmer for 30 minutes. Season to taste.

Serves 4
***

CRISPY MUSHROOM CRUMBLE

Oil 2 tbsp (30 ml)
Onion, sliced 8 oz (225 g)
Garlic clove, crushed 1
Dried marjoram 1 tsp (5 ml)
Dried thyme 1 tsp (5 ml)
Wholemeal flour 1 oz (25 g)
Tomatoes, sliced 8 oz (225 g)
Mushrooms, sliced 1 lb (450 g)
Red wine 6 tbsp (90 ml)
Tomato purée 1 tbsp (15 ml)
Soya sauce 1 tbsp (15 ml)
Vegetable extract 1 tsp (5 ml)
Molasses 1 tsp (5 ml)
Salt & pepper to taste

TOPPING
Toasted wholemeal breadcrumbs 3 oz (75 g)
Rolled oats 1 oz (25 g)
Sesame seeds, toasted 1 oz (25 g)
Sunflower seeds, toasted 1 oz (25 g)
Cheddar cheese, grated (optional) 4 oz (100 g)
Parsley, chopped 2 tbsp (30 ml)
Butter 1 oz (25 g)

Heat the oil and sauté the onion, garlic and herbs until
the onion is transparent. Stir in the flour and cook for
2–3 minutes. Add the remaining ingredients, stir well
and simmer for 15–20 minutes. Season to taste.

Transfer the mixture to an ovenproof dish.
Combine all the ingredients for the topping. Rub in
the butter and sprinkle the mixture over the
mushrooms. Bake at 375°F/190°C/gas mark 5 for 20–
25 minutes.

Serves 4
***

BOMBAY SWEDE

Swede, diced 2 lb (900 g)
Butter 1 oz (25 g), Oil 2 tbsp (30 ml)
Onion, sliced 8 oz (225 g)
Garlic cloves, crushed 2
Curry powder 1 tsp (5 ml)
Ground ginger ¼ tsp (1.25 ml)
Ground coriander 1 tsp (5 ml)
Ground cumin ½ tsp (2.5 ml)
Turmeric ¼ tsp (1.25 ml)
Ground cloves, a pinch
Chilli powder, a pinch
Wholemeal flour 1 oz (25 g)
Tomato juice ¾ pt (450 ml)
Tomato purée 2 tbsp (30 ml)
Tomatoes, sliced 8 oz (225 g)
Cooking apple, diced 6 oz (175 g)
Desiccated coconut, toasted 2 oz (50 g)
Sultanas 3 oz (75 g)
Green pepper, deseeded and sliced 1
Red pepper, deseeded and sliced 1
Salt & pepper to taste

Steam or cook the swede in boiling water for about 30 minutes until tender. Drain, mash with the butter and season. Heat the oil and sauté the onion, garlic and spices until the onion is soft. Stir in the flour and cook for 1 minute.

Add the tomatoes, purée and juice. Simmer for 10 minutes. Add the remaining ingredients and simmer covered for a further 15 minutes, stirring occasionally. If necessary, add ¼ pt (150 ml) of the cooking water from the swede. Season to taste.

Transfer the mashed swede to a serving dish and top with the spiced vegetable mixture.

Serves 4–6

AUBERGINE, MUSHROOM & POTATO STEW

Oil 2 tbsp (30 ml)
Butter 1 oz (25 g)
Garlic cloves, crushed 2
Aubergine, cut into large dice 12 oz (350 g)
Button mushrooms 12 oz (350 g)
New (or small) potatoes, thickly sliced 1½ lb (675 g)
Bayleaf 1
Sprigs of thyme, a few
Vegetable stock ¼ pt (150 ml)
Dry white wine ¼ pt (150 ml)
Salt & pepper to taste

Heat the oil and butter and sauté the garlic, aubergine and mushrooms until just tender. Add the remaining ingredients, cover and simmer for 20 minutes.

Season to taste.

Serves 4
***

POTATO & TURNIP DAUPHINOISE

Serve this with a green salad.

Baby turnips, thinly sliced 1 lb (450 g)
Potatoes, thinly sliced 1 lb (450 g)
Butter 1 oz (25 g)
Garlic cloves, sliced 2
Single cream ½ pt (300 ml)
Gruyère cheese, grated 2 oz (50 g)
Cheddar cheese, grated 2 oz (50 g)
Salt & pepper to taste

Place the turnips and potatoes in a large pan and just cover with cold water. Bring to a fast boil. Remove from the heat immediately and drain well.

Butter an ovenproof dish and layer up the vegetables with the garlic, seasoning generously between the layers. Dot with the remaining butter.

Pour the single cream over and sprinkle with the cheese. Bake in a bain marie (covered dish, standing in roasting tin of water) in the oven at 400°F (200°C) gas mark 6 for 1–1¼ hours until tender.

Serves 4

TOFU TEMPURA

Smoked tofu 8 oz (225 g)
Soya sauce 2 tbsp (30 ml)
Honey 1 tbsp (15 ml)
Root ginger, grated 1 tbsp (15 ml)
Garlic cloves, crushed 2
Tahini paste 2 tbsp (30 ml)
Water 4 tbsp (60 ml)

BATTER
Brown rice flour 2 oz (50 g)
Wholemeal flour 1 oz (25 g)
Baking powder 1 tsp (5 ml)
Wholewheat semolina 1 tsp (5 ml)
Iced water 4 fl oz (100 ml)
Oil for deep frying

Cut the tofu into 8 even slices. Halve each piece. Place on a clean tea towel, cover with another tea towel and then a board or tray. Top with a heavy weight and leave for 30 minutes to drain out any excess moisture.

Mix together the remaining ingredients. Arrange the tofu in a single layer. Cover with the soya mixture, cover and leave to marinate for several hours – up to 24 hours.

Remove from the marinate and drain on absorbent paper. Toss carefully in 1 oz (25 g) of rice flour.

For the batter whisk the ingredients together. Dip the tofu slices in the batter, then drop immediately into hot oil. Fry until crisp and golden. Drain on absorbent paper.

Serve at once with natural yoghourt flavoured with grated cucumber.

Serves 4

GREEN VEGETABLE QUICHE

Wholemeal pastry, made using wholemeal flour
(see chart p. 8) 5 oz (150 g)
Butter 1 oz (25 g)
Courgette, thickly sliced 6 oz (175 g)
Spring onions, sliced 1 bunch
Asparagus spears, cooked 12
Stilton cheese, grated 2 oz (50 g)
Free-range eggs 3
Single cream 6 fl oz (175 ml)
Salt & pepper to taste

Roll out the pastry and use to line an 8 in (20 cm) deep French fluted flan tin. Bake blind at 400°F (200°C) gas mark 6 for 10 minutes. Reduce the heat to 375°F (190°C) gas mark 5.

Melt the butter and sauté the courgettes and then the spring onions until just tender. Slice the asparagus, leaving the tips about 2 in (5 cm) long.

Beat together the cheese, eggs, cream and seasoning. Pour the mixture into the flan case. Sprinkle with the sliced asparagus.

Arrange the courgette slices in a circle around the outside of the pastry case. Arrange the asparagus tips in the centre with the spring onions. Bake for about 40 minutes until the filling is just set. Serve warm or cold.

Serves 4–6
***

MIXED GRAIN & WALNUT PUDDING

A substantial and nutritious dish for a family meal.

Oil 2 tbsp (30 ml)
Onion, chopped 4 oz (100 g)
Garlic clove, crushed 1
Carrot, diced 4 oz (100 g)
Celery stick, diced 1
Long grain brown rice 3 oz (75 g)
Vegetable stock 1¼–1½ pt (750–900 ml)
Red lentils 3 oz (75 g)
Flaked millet 2 oz (50 g)
Cornmeal 1 oz (25 g)
Dried sage 1 tsp (5 ml)
Celery seeds 1 tsp (5 ml)
Soya sauce 1 tbsp (15 ml)
Walnuts, chopped 2 oz (50 g)
Sunflower seeds 1 oz (25 g)
Fresh wholemeal breadcrumbs 2 oz (50 g)
Salt & pepper to taste

Heat the oil and sauté the onion, garlic, carrot and celery until the onion is transparent. Add the rice and half the stock, cover and simmer for 15 minutes.

Add the lentils and half the remaining stock. Cover and simmer for a further 15 minutes. Add the millet, cornmeal, sage, celery seeds and soya sauce. Add the remaining stock and simmer very gently, stirring frequently for 30 minutes. Add the remaining ingredients and season to taste.

Transfer to a buttered, ovenproof serving dish and bake at 400°F (200°C) gas mark 6 for 20–30 minutes.

Serve with spinach sauce or rich brown onion sauce (see p. 84 or p. 86).

Serves 4–6
***

FESTIVE CRANBERRY TERRINE

A stunning centre piece for the Christmas table.

Wholemeal pastry, made using wholemeal flour (see chart p. 8) 9 oz (275 g)
Mixed grain and walnut pudding mixture (see p. 29) 1 quantity
Agar flakes 1½ tsp (7.5 ml)
Cranberries 2 oz (50 g)
Unrefined brown sugar 1 tbsp (15 ml)
Walnut halves, roasted 10
Flat leaf parsley sprigs to garnish

Roll out the pastry and use to line the base and sides of a 2 lb (900 g) loaf tin. Neaten the top edge. Allow the mixed grain and walnut pudding mixture to go cold and use to fill the pastry case. Cover and bake at 400°F (200°C) gas mark 6 for 50 minutes to 1 hour. Leave to go cold. Remove from the tin.

Place the agar flakes in a saucepan with ¼ pt (150 ml) water. Bring to the boil, then simmer gently for 1–2 minutes until dissolved. Take 2 tbsp (30 ml) of this liquid and place in a saucepan with the cranberries and sugar. Cool the remaining liquid. Cook over a gentle heat until the cranberries just 'pop'. Cool slightly and arrange the cranberries on the surface of the terrine. Brush with their cooled liquid. Dip the walnut halves and parsley sprigs in the cooled agar liquid and arrange beside the cranberries. Chill the remaining liquid until just on the point of setting then brush over the whole surface to glaze.

Serves 8–10
*** without topping.

POLISH CABBAGE STEW

Butter 2 oz (50 g)
Onion, sliced 12 oz (350 g)
White cabbage, cut into 8 wedges 2½–3 lb (1.1–1.4 kg)
Small apples, quartered and cored 12 oz (350 g)
Tomatoes, quartered 8 oz (225 g)
Bayleaves 2
Cider or wine vinegar 1 tbsp (15 ml)
Smoked tofu, cubed 8 oz (225 g)
Salt & pepper to taste
Chopped parsley to garnish

Melt the butter in a large flameproof casserole and sauté the onion until transparent. Arrange the wedges of cabbage on top of the onion. Add the apples, tomatoes, bay leaves and cider vinegar. Cover and simmer very gently for 1¾ hours.

Add the smoked tofu and seasoning and cook for a further 95 minutes.

Sprinkle with chopped parsley before serving. Serve with jacket potatoes.

Serves 4–6
***

CHEESY AUBERGINE LAYER

New (or small) potatoes 1¼ lb (550 g)
Aubergines, sliced 1¼ lb (550 g)
Dried basil ½ tsp (2.5 ml)
Dried oregano ½ tsp (2.5 ml)
Tomato sauce (see p. 85) 1 quantity
Cheddar cheese, grated 6 oz (175 g)
Salt & pepper to taste

Steam the potatoes for about 15 minutes until just tender. Cut into thick slices.

Steam the aubergine slices with the basil and oregano for 10–12 minutes until just tender. In a buttered, ovenproof dish, layer up the potatoes, aubergines, tomato sauce and cheese, seasoning between each layer and finishing with the cheese.

Bake at 400°F (200°C) gas mark 6 for 20–25 minutes until bubbling and golden.

Serves 4
***

MIXED VEGETABLES
IN CHEESE SAUCE

Potatoes, cut in large dice 12 oz (350 g)
Baby carrots 8 oz (225 g)
Leek, thickly sliced 6 oz (175 g)
Courgettes, thickly sliced 6 oz (175 g)
Broccoli, cut into florets 4 oz (100 g)
Cheese sauce (see p. 86) 1 quantity
Parsley, chopped 6 tbsp (90 ml)
Salt & pepper to taste

Steam or cook the potatoes and carrots in boiling water for 5 minutes. Add the leek, courgettes and broccoli and cook for a further 5 minutes until all the vegetables are just tender. Drain well.

Combine with the remaining ingredients, season to taste and warm through gently to reheat.

Serve with freshly cooked rice.

Serves 4
***

VEGETABLE PASTIES

Hot water crust pastry (see p. 8) 1 quantity
Mushrooms, finely diced 3 oz (75 g)
Onion, finely diced 3 oz (75 g)
Root vegetables, such as potato, swede, turnip, carrot,
kohlrabi, finely diced 10 oz (300 g)
Salt ½ tsp (2.5 ml)
Pepper ¼ tsp (1.25 ml)
Beaten egg to glaze

Roll out the pastry and cut out eight 7 in (18 cm) rounds.

Combine all the vegetables with the salt and pepper. Mix well and divide between the pastry rounds. Damp the edges with water, then fold over and seal the edges well. Crimp the edges to give a decorative effect. Cut 2 slashes in each pasty, brush with beaten egg and bake at 400°F (200°C) gas mark 6 for 15 minutes.

Reduce the heat to 350°F (180°C) gas mark 4 and cook for a further 30 minutes.

Serve warm with Rich brown onion sauce, or cold (see p. 86).

Makes 8
***

SAVOURY MILLET

Millet 6 oz (175 g)
Oil 2 tbsp (30 ml)
Onion, sliced 4 oz (100 g)
Garlic cloves, sliced 2
Dried mixed herbs 1 tsp (5 ml)
Dried basil 1 tsp (5 ml)
Dried sage 1 tsp (5 ml)
Paprika ½ tsp (2.5 ml)
Cayenne, a pinch
Carrot, cut into large dice
Celery, sliced 4 oz (100 g)
Green pepper, deseeded and sliced 1
Tomatoes 14 oz can (400 g can)
Soya sauce 1 tbsp (15 ml)
Lemon juice 1 tbsp (15 ml)
Spinach, shredded 4 oz (100 g)
Salt & pepper to taste
Parsley, chopped 4 tbsp (60 ml)

Cook the millet in 1½ pt (900 ml) of boiling water for about 25 minutes until tender and all the water has been absorbed.

Heat the oil and sauté the onion until transparent. Add the garlic, herbs, spices, carrot, celery and green pepper and sauté for 5 minutes. Add the tomatoes, soya sauce and lemon juice. Cover and simmer for 15–20 minutes until tender. Stir in the spinach until just wilted, then stir in the cooked millet, reheat gently and season to taste. Stir in the parsley.

Serves 4

LENTIL SAVOURY

Red lentils 8 oz (225 g)
Oil 1 tbsp (15 ml)
Onion, sliced 4 oz (100 g)
Garlic cloves, sliced 2
Ground bay leaf ¼ tsp (1.25 ml)
Dried thyme ½ tsp (2.5 ml)
Dried rosemary ½ tsp (2.5 ml)
Carrots, cut in large dice 8 oz (225 g)
Mushrooms, sliced 4 oz (100 g)
Tomatoes, quartered 8 oz (225 g)
Vegetable stock ¾ pt (450 ml)
Tomato purée 1 tbsp (15 ml)
Soya sauce 1 tbsp (15 l)
Salt & pepper to taste

Cover the lentils with cold water and leave to soak whilst the vegetables are cooking.

Heat the oil and sauté the onion until transparent. Add the garlic, herbs, carrot and mushrooms and sauté for 5 minutes.

Add the remaining ingredients. Drain the lentils and add to the pan. Cover and simmer for 20 minutes until the lentils are just cooked. Season to taste.

Serves 4
***

PASTA WITH WALNUT & MUSHROOM SAUCE

Oil 4 tbsp (60 ml)
Onion, chopped 4 oz (100 g)
Garlic cloves, sliced 2
Ground cinnamon ¼ tsp (1.25 ml)
Ground allspice ¼ tsp (1.25 ml)
Ground ginger ¼ tsp (1.25 ml)
Walnuts 4 oz (100 g)
Mushrooms, sliced 12 oz (350 g)
Tomatoes, sliced 8 oz (225 g)
Tomato purée 1 tbsp (15 ml)
Vegetable extract 1 tsp (5 ml)
Unrefined brown sugar 2 tsp (10 ml)
Soya sauce 1 tbsp (15 ml)
Red wine ¼ pt (150 ml)
Salt & pepper to taste
Wholewheat pasta shapes 9–10 oz (250–300 g)
Chopped parsley to garnish

Heat half the oil and sauté the onion, garlic and spices until the onion is transparent. Heat the remaining oil and sauté the walnuts until golden. Drain carefully.

Add the mushrooms to the pan and sauté.

Add about half the walnuts and about one quarter of the mushrooms to the onion mixture with the remaining ingredients except the pasta. Cover and simmer for 15 minutes, then blend in a liquidizer or food processor.

Add the remaining walnuts and mushroom slices to the sauce and season to taste.

Cook the pasta according to packet directions. Drain well.

Reheat the sauce, adding up to ¼ pt (150 ml) vegetable stock if necessary to give a good consistency. Serve the pasta with the sauce poured over. Alternatively, mix the pasta with the sauce before serving.

Sprinkle with chopped parsley.

Variation
Add ¼ pt (150 ml) single cream instead of the vegetable stock when reheating the sauce.

Serves 4

RATATOUILLE

Delicious on its own, but also good as a filling for pastry and pancakes.

Olive oil 4 tbsp (60 ml)
Onion, sliced 4 oz (100 g)
Garlic cloves, sliced 2
Aubergines, diced 8 oz (225 g)
Courgettes, cut into large dice 8 oz (225 g)
Red pepper, deseeded and sliced 1
Tomatoes, sliced 8 oz (225 g)
Tomato purée 2 tbsp (30 ml)
Sprigs of thyme, a few
Sprigs of rosemary, a few
Salt & pepper to taste
Freshly chopped herbs, such as parsley, basil and oregano 2 tbsp (30 ml)

Heat the oil and sauté the onion and garlic until transparent. Add the aubergine and sauté for 5 minutes. Add the courgettes and pepper and sauté for 5 minutes. Add the remaining ingredients except the chopped herbs. Cover and simmer for 20 minutes or until tender. Season to taste and stir in the fresh herbs. Serve with freshly-cooked rice or noodles.

Serves 4
***

RATATOUILLE PASTIES

Hot water crust pastry (see p. 8) 1 quantity
Cold ratatouille (see p. 37) 1 quantity
Beaten egg to glaze

Roll out the pastry and cut out eight 7 in (18 cm) rounds.

Divide the cold ratatouille mixture between the pastry rounds. Damp the edges with water, then bring the edges up to meet in the centre and seal well. Crimp the edges to give a decorative effect. Cut 2 slashes in each pasty.

Brush with beaten egg and bake at 400°F (200°C) gas mark 6 for 20–25 minutes until golden brown.

Serve hot or cold.
***

BUTTERBEANS WITH SPINACH SAUCE

Butterbeans, soaked overnight 8 oz (225 g)
Baby carrots or carrots, thickly sliced 12 oz (350 g)
Spinach sauce (see p. 84) 1 quantity
Salt & pepper to taste

Drain the beans, then bring to the boil in fresh water. Boil for 10 minutes, then reduce the heat and simmer for about 50 minutes or until tender. Drain.

Steam the carrots for about 10 minutes until just tender.

Combine the ingredients, warm through over a gentle heat. Season to taste.

Serves 4
***

BUCKWHEAT CASSEROLE

Roasting enhances the flavour of the buckwheat. It is now available ready roasted in most health food shops; however, instructions for roasting are given below.

Buckwheat 6 oz (175 g)
Free-range egg, beaten 1
Butter 2 oz (50 g)
Celery sticks, sliced 4
Onion, diced 1
Carrots, diced 8 oz (225 g)
Vegetable stock ¾–1 pt (450–600 ml)
Wholemeal flour 1 oz (25 g)
Milk ¾–1 pt (450–600 ml)
Parsley, chopped 4 tbsp (60 ml)
Fresh chives, chopped 2 tbsp (30 ml)
Pecans, toasted and roughly chopped 4 oz (100 g)
Salt & pepper to taste

Mix the buckwheat and beaten egg and dry fry over gentle heat until golden.

Melt half the butter and sauté the celery, onion and carrot until the onion is transparent. Add the buckwheat and vegetable stock. Cover and simmer for 20 minutes.

Melt the remaining butter, stir in the flour and cook for 1–2 minutes. Stir in ¾ pt (450 ml) milk and cook, stirring, until thickened. Stir in the herbs and season to taste.

Combine the buckwheat mixture with the herb sauce and pecan nuts. Reheat gently and season to taste, adding extra milk if necessary.

Serves 4–6
***

CRANKS MOUSSAKA

Aubergines, diced 1 lb (450 g)
Courgettes, sliced 8 oz (225 g)
Tomato sauce (see p. 85) ½ quantity
Assorted nuts, such as peanuts, walnuts, almonds
4 oz (100 g)
Salt & pepper to taste
Cheese sauce (see p. 86) ½ quantity

Steam the aubergine for 10 minutes. Steam the courgettes for 5 minutes.

Layer up the aubergines and courgettes, seasoning between each layer with the tomato sauce and nuts.

Top with the cheese sauce and bake at 400°F (200°C) gas mark 6 for 25–30 minutes until golden and bubbling.

Serves 4
***

WHOLEWHEAT FRICASSEE

Wholewheat berries, soaked overnight 8 oz (225 g)
Celery, sliced 6 oz (175 g)
Leek, cut into 1 in (2.5 cm) lengths 6 oz (175 g)
Tomatoes, quartered 8 oz (225 g)
Cheese sauce (see p. 86) 1 quantity
Salt & pepper to taste

Drain the wholewheat then bring to the boil in fresh water. Simmer for 30–35 minutes until just tender. Drain.

Steam the celery and leek for 5–10 minutes, then mix all the ingredients together. Warm through over a gentle heat.

Season to taste.

Serves 4
***

VEGETABLE ALMOND CRUMBLE

Potatoes, cut into large dice 12 oz (350 g)
Celery, sliced 8 oz (225 g)
Leek, cut into 1 in (2.5 cm) lengths 8 oz (225 g)
Cheese sauce (see p. 86) ½ quantity
Porridge oats 2 oz (50 g)
Toasted wholemeal breadcrumbs 2 oz (50 g)
Flaked almonds, toasted 2 oz (50 g)
Butter 2 oz (50 g)
Salt & pepper to taste

Steam the potatoes and celery for 5 minutes. Add the leek and steam for a further 5 minutes until all the vegetables are just tender.

Mix the vegetables with the cheese sauce, season to taste and transfer to an ovenproof dish.

Mix the oats, breadcrumbs and almonds and rub in the butter. Sprinkle over the vegetables and bake at 400°F (200°C) gas mark 6 for 25–30 minutes.

Serves 4
***

HARICOT BEAN & VEGETABLE PIE

Haricot beans, soaked overnight 6 oz (175 g)
Butter 2 oz (50 g)
Onion, sliced 6 oz (175 g)
Garlic cloves, crushed 2
Dried basil 1 tsp (5 ml)
Dried mixed herbs 1 tsp (5 ml)
Tomato juice 1 pt (600 ml)
Tomato purée 2 tbsp (30 ml)
Soya sauce 1 tbsp (15 ml)
Carrots, sliced 8 oz (225 g)
Celery, sliced 8 oz (225 g)
Courgette, sliced 4 oz (100 g)
Potatoes 1½ lb (675 g)
Cheddar cheese, grated 2 oz (50 g)
Milk 4 tbsp (60 ml)
Parsley, chopped 2 tbsp (30 ml)
Salt & pepper to taste

Drain the beans, then bring to the boil in fresh water. Boil for 10 minutes then reduce the heat and simmer for about 50 minutes or until tender. Drain.

Melt half the butter and sauté the onion, garlic and herbs until the onion is transparent. Add the tomato juice, tomato purée and soya sauce. Bring to the boil, add the carrots and simmer for 10 minutes. Add the celery and courgettes and simmer for a further 10 minutes or until tender. Stir in the cooked beans and season to taste.

Steam or cook the potatoes in boiling water. Drain well and mash with the remaining butter, cheese, milk, parsley and seasoning. Spoon the bean mixture into an ovenproof serving dish. Top with the potato mixture and reheat in the oven at 400°F (200°C) gas mark 6 for 20–30 minutes.

Serves 4–6
***

CRANKS CASSOULET

Haricot beans, soaked overnight 8 oz (225 g)
Tomato sauce (see p. 85) 1 quantity
Carrots, baby or sliced 6 oz (175 g)
Courgettes, large dice 8 oz (225 g)
Red pepper, deseeded and sliced 1
Green pepper, deseeded and sliced 1
Salt & pepper to taste

Drain the beans then bring to the boil in fresh water.
Boil for 10 minutes, then reduce the heat and simmer
for about 50 minutes or until tender. Drain.

Place the tomato sauce in a large saucepan. Add the
carrots and cook for 10 minutes. Add the remaining
vegetables and simmer for a further 10 minutes.

Add the cooked beans and simmer gently until the
vegetables are tender and the beans warmed.

Season to taste.

Serves 4
***

43

PIMENTO PIE

Oil 4 tbsp (60 ml)
Onion, sliced 6 oz (175 g)
Ground bayleaf ½ tsp (2.5 ml)
Dried thyme 1 tsp (5 ml)
Dried mixed herbs 1 tsp (5 ml)
Red peppers, deseeded and sliced 2
Mushrooms, sliced 6 oz (175 g)
Celery, sliced 4 oz (100 g)
Wholewheat flour 1 oz (25 g)
Tomatoes 14 oz can (400 g can)
Vegetable stock ¼ pt (150 ml)
Tomato purée 2 tbsp (30 ml)
Soya sauce 1 tbsp (15 ml)
Vegetable extract 1 tsp (5 ml)
Parsley, chopped 2 tbsp (30 ml)

Topping: *Potatoes 1½ lb (675 g)*
Butter 1 oz (25 g)
Milk 4 tbsp (60 ml)
Salt & pepper to taste

Heat the oil and sauté the onion and herbs together until the onion is transparent. Add the red pepper, mushrooms and celery and sauté for 5 minutes. Stir in the flour and cook, stirring for 1–2 minutes. Add the can of tomatoes, vegetable stock, tomato purée, soya sauce and vegetable extract. Cover and simmer for 15–20 minutes until tender. Stir in the parsley and season to taste.

Steam or cook the potatoes in boiling water for about 20 minutes until tender. Drain and mash with the butter and milk. Season to taste.

Transfer the pepper mixture to an ovenproof serving dish. Top with the mashed potato and bake in the oven at 400°F (200°C) gas mark 6 for 20–30 minutes.

Serves 4
***

SWEDE TOPPED CASSEROLE

Oil 2 tbsp (30 ml)
Onion, sliced 4 oz (100 g)
Garlic cloves, crushed 2
Dried oregano and basil 1 tsp (5 ml) each
Ground bayleaf ¼ tsp (1.25 ml)
Tomatoes, sliced 1 lb (450 g)
Tomato purée 2 tbsp (30 ml)
Vegetable stock ½ pt (300 ml)
Potato, cut into large dice 6 oz (175 g)
Carrot, sliced 12 oz (350 g)
Celery, sliced 4 oz (100 g)
Green pepper, deseeded and sliced 1
Courgette, cut into large dice 8 oz (225 g)
Swede or parsnips, diced 1½ lb (675 g)
Butter 1 oz (25 g)
Ground nutmeg, a pinch
Flaked almonds 2 oz (50 g)
Cheddar cheese, grated 2 oz (50 g)
Salt & pepper to taste

Heat the oil and sauté the onion, garlic and herbs until the onion is transparent. Add the tomatoes, tomato purée and stock and simmer covered for 10 minutes. Add the potatoes and carrots and simmer for 15 minutes, then stir in the remaining vegetables, except the swede. Cover and simmer for a further 15–20 minutes until the vegetables are tender. Season. Steam or cook the swede in boiling water for about 30 minutes until tender. Drain well and mash with the butter. Season to taste with nutmeg, salt and pepper.

Transfer the vegetable mixture to an ovenproof serving dish. Top with the swede mixture. Sprinkle with the almonds and cheese and bake in the oven at 400°F (200°C) gas mark 6 for 20–30 minutes.

Serves 4–6
***

CAULIFLOWER & COURGETTE NIÇOISE

Serve this for a light lunch with wholemeal garlic bread.

Cauliflower florets 1 lb (450 g)
Courgettes, thickly sliced 1 lb (450 g)
Provençale sauce (see p. 87) 1 quantity
Tomato juice ¼ pt (150 ml)
Sesame seeds, toasted 2 tbsp (30 ml)
Salt & pepper to taste

Steam the cauliflower florets for about 10 minutes and the courgettes for about 5 minutes until just tender, but still crisp.

Warm the provençale sauce with the extra tomato juice. Stir in the vegetables and season to taste.

Sprinkle with sesame seeds.

Serves 4

MACARONI & VEGETABLE CHEESE

Wholewheat macaroni spirals 6 oz (175 g)
Carrots, sliced 8 oz (225 g)
Leeks, cut into 1 in (2.5 cm) pieces 6 oz (175 g)
Butter 1 oz (25 g)
Mushrooms, sliced 8 oz (225 g)
Cheese sauce (see p. 86) 1 quantity
Salt & pepper to taste

Cook the macaroni in boiling water according to the packet directions. Drain.

Steam the carrots for 10 minutes, add the leeks and cook for a further 5–7 minutes until just tender.

Melt the butter and sauté the mushrooms. Warm the cheese sauce, stir in the pasta and vegetables and season to taste.

Reheat gently.

Serves 4
***

BEANS & PASTA WITH
CHILLI SAUCE

Kidney or haricot beans, soaked overnight 8 oz (225 g)
Wholewheat pasta spirals 3 oz (75 g)
Oil 2 tbsp (30 ml)
Onion, sliced 4 oz (100 g)
Garlic cloves, crushed 2
Ground cumin ½ tsp (2.5 ml)
Dried thyme ½ tsp (2.5 ml)
Fresh chillies, deseeded and sliced 2
Tomato juice ½ pt (300 ml)
Tomatoes 14 oz can (400 g can)
Tomato purée 1 tbsp (15 ml)
Soya sauce 1 tbsp (15ml)
Aubergines, diced 4 oz (100 g)
Courgettes, sliced 4 oz (100 g)
Green pepper, deseeded and sliced 1
Salt & pepper to taste

Drain the beans then bring to the boil in fresh water.
Boil for 15 minutes then reduce the heat and simmer
for 50–60 minutes or until tender. Drain.

Cook the pasta in boiling water according to packet
directions. Drain.

Heat the oil and sauté the onion until transparent.
Add the garlic, cumin, thyme and chillies and sauté
for 2–3 minutes.

Stir in the tomato juice, canned tomatoes, tomato
purée and soya sauce. Stir well. Add the aubergine
and simmer, covered for 10 minutes. Add the
courgettes and green pepper and simmer for a further
10 minutes.

Stir in the beans and pasta, season to taste and
reheat gently.

Serves 4
***

Wheatberry, Nut & Broccoli Ragout, page 16
Chilli Beanpot, page 17
Beansprout & Tofu Latkes, page 10

Bombay Swede, page 24
Layered Mediterranean Vegetable Pudding, page 14
Cauliflower & Courgette Niçoise, page 46

Polish Cabbage Stew, page 31
Aubergine, Mushroom & Potato Stew, page 25
Savoury Millet, page 34

Vegetable Almond Crumble, page 41
Beetroot, Apple & Potato Ragout, page 72
Mixed Vegetables with Satay Sauce, page 50

Raised Vegetable & Nut Pie, page 80
Cinderella Roast (pumpkin), page 52
Sunflower Popovers, page 60

Spinach, Lentil & Tofu Roulade, page 77
Cranks Deep Pan Pizza, page 68
Traditional Tortilla, page 65

Paella – Cranks Style, page 71
Vegetable & Fruit Couscous, page 67
Green & White Terrine, page 76

Festive Cranberry Terrine, page 30
Ratatouille Pasties, page 38
Green Vegetable Quiche, page 28

CREAMY MUSHROOM RAGOUT

For this dish, try using some of the more unusual mushrooms such as oyster, chestnut and shiitake.

Butter 2 oz (50 g)
Onion, sliced 4 oz (100 g)
Garlic cloves, crushed 2
Ground bayleaf ¼ tsp (1.25 ml)
Dried thyme ½ tsp (2.5 ml)
Dried tarragon ½ tsp (2.5 ml)
Dried mixed herbs ¼ tsp (1.25 ml)
Ground ginger ½ tsp (2.5 ml)
Wholemeal flour 1 oz (25 g)
Vegetable extract 1 tsp (5 ml)
Soya sauce 1 tbsp (15 ml)
Dry red wine ¼ pt (150 ml)
Vegetable stock ¼ pt (150 ml)
Carrots, diced 4 oz (100 g)
Celery, sliced 6 oz (175 g)
Mushrooms, sliced 1 lb (450 g)
Soured cream ¼ pt (150 ml)
Salt & pepper to taste

Melt the butter and sauté the onion and garlic until transparent. Stir in the herbs, spices and flour and cook for 1–2 minutes. Add the next 6 ingredients and bring to the boil. Cover and simmer for 10 minutes. Add the mushrooms and simmer for a further 15 minutes, stirring occasionally. Remove from the heat, stir in the soured cream and season to taste.

Serve with freshly cooked rice or pasta mixed with chopped parsley.

Serves 4
***

MIXED VEGETABLES WITH SATAY SAUCE

Oil 3 tbsp (45 ml)
Onion, sliced 6 oz (175 g)
Garlic cloves, sliced 3
Chilli powder ¼ tsp (1.25 ml)
Crunchy peanut butter 8 oz (225 g)
Cider vinegar 4 tsp (20 ml)
Pineapple juice ½ pt (300 ml)
Tomato juice ¼ pt (150 ml)
Honey and soya sauce 1 tbsp (15 ml) each
Medium pineapple, peeled and cut into small dice
¼ (12–14 oz) (350–400 g)
Carrots, sliced 4 oz (100 g)
Parsnip, diced 4 oz (100 g)
Broccoli, cut into florets 4 oz (100 g)
Butter 1 oz (25 g)
Courgettes, sliced 8 oz (225 g)
Smoked tofu, cut into small slices 8 oz (225 g)
Salt & pepper to taste

For the sauce, heat 2 tbsp (30 ml) oil and sauté the onion and 2 garlic cloves with the chilli powder until the onion is soft. Stir in the peanut butter, cider vinegar, pineapple juice, tomato juice, honey and soya sauce. Heat gently, add the pineapple and season to taste. Steam the carrots and parsnips for 6–7 minutes. Add the broccoli and steam for a further 3–4 minutes. Heat the butter with the remaining oil. Sauté the courgettes with the remaining garlic until lightly golden. Add the tofu and sauté gently. Stir in the steamed vegetables. Season to taste.

Warm the sauce and pour into a serving dish. Spoon the vegetable mixture on top.

Serves 4

BUCKWHEAT & EGG FLORENTINE

Rich in minerals and vitamins, this recipe is a Cranks variation of the traditional dish. Serve with a tomato salad.

Buckwheat 6 oz (175 g)
Butter 1 oz (25 g)
Oil 1 tbsp (15 ml)
Mushrooms, sliced 4 oz (100 g)
Spinach, roughly chopped 1 lb (450 g)
Ground nutmeg, a pinch
Free-range eggs, hard boiled and shelled 6
Cheese sauce (see p. 86) 1 quantity
Fresh wholemeal breadcrumbs 4 tbsp (60 ml)
Salt & pepper to taste

Cook the buckwheat in boiling water or vegetable stock for about 15 minutes until tender. Drain well.

Heat the butter and oil and sauté the mushrooms. Add the spinach and cook over high heat until the spinach has wilted and no liquid remains. Season with nutmeg, salt and pepper to taste. Stir in the buckwheat.

Transfer to an overproof serving dish. Halve or quarter the eggs and arrange on top. Cover with the cheese sauce and sprinkle with breadcrumbs.

Bake at 375°F (190°C) gas mark 5 for about 25 minutes until golden and bubbling.

Serves 4

CINDERELLA ROAST

Whole pumpkin 3½–4 lb
Dried chestnuts, soaked overnight 4 oz (100 g)
Butter 1 oz (25 g)
Oil 1 tbsp (15 ml)
Onion, chopped 4 oz (100 g)
Celery, sliced 2 oz (50 g)
Mushrooms, sliced 4 oz (100 g)
Fresh wholemeal breadcrumbs 8 oz (225 g)
Hazelnuts, toasted and chopped 2 oz (50 g)
Dried sage 2 tsp (10 ml)
Vegetable extract 1 tsp (5 ml)
Salt & pepper to taste

Using a zig-zag movement, cut the top off the pumpkin. Remove and discard the seeds and membrane. Replace the lid and bake the pumpkin at 350°F (180°C) gas mark 4 for 1 hour.

Cook the chestnuts in boiling water for about 45 minutes until tender. Drain and reserve ¼ pt (150 ml) cooking liquid.

Heat the butter and oil and sauté the onion and celery until the onion is transparent. Add the mushrooms and sauté. Stir in the remaining ingredients. Remove from the heat and stir in the chestnuts, with their liquid.

Carefully scoop out about 1 lb (450 g) pumpkin flesh and roughly chop it. Add to the chestnut mixture and season generously.

Pile the mixture back into the pumpkin, packing it down firmly. Replace the lid and bake for a further 30–45 minutes until tender.

Serve cut into wedges with red wine sauce or lemon sauce (see p. 89 or p. 88).

Variation
Chestnut and parsnip mix roast. Omit the pumpkin and substitute 1 lb (450 g) cooked parsnip in the nut roast mix. Transfer to a buttered ovenproof dish and bake for 45 minutes to reheat.

Serves 6–8
***

COURGETTE & CREAM CHEESE ROAST

Rich and delicious – serve it for a special occasion.

Butter 2 oz (50 g)
Onion, chopped 12 oz (350 g)
Courgettes, sliced 1 lb (450 g)
Carrot, grated 4 oz (150 g)
Cream cheese 8 oz (225 g)
Desiccated coconut, toasted 2 oz (50 g)
Cashew nuts, toasted 4 oz (100 g)
Fresh wholemeal breadcrumbs 8 oz (225 g)
Fresh marjoram, chopped 1 tbsp (15 ml)
Salt & pepper to taste

Melt the butter and sauté the onion until transparent. Add the courgettes and cook until just tender. Stir in the carrot and cook for 1–2 minutes. Combine all the ingredients, mix well and season generously.

Butter and line the base of a 2 lb (900 g) loaf tin. Press the mixture into the tin, cover and bake at 375°F (190°C) gas mark 5 for 45 minutes. Remove the cover 10 minutes before the end of cooking. Unmould onto a serving plate and cut into thick slices. Serve with lemon sauce or tomato sauce (see p. 88 or p. 85).

Serves 6–8
***

WILD MUSHROOM QUICHE

Wholemeal pastry made using wholemeal flour
(see chart p. 8) 5 oz (150 g)
Butter 1 oz (25 g)
Shallots, finely chopped 1 oz (25 g)
Wild mushrooms, roughly chopped 6 oz (175 g)
Cream cheese 6 oz (175 g)
Single cream ¼ pt (150 ml)
Free-range eggs 2
Fresh chives, chopped 2 tbsp (30 ml)
Fresh tarragon, chopped 2 tsp (10 ml)
Coarse grain mustard 1 tsp (5 ml)
Salt & pepper to taste

Roll out the pastry and use to line a deep-sided 8 in
(20 cm) French fluted flan tin. Bake 'blind' in the oven
at 400°F (200°C) gas mark 6 for 10 minutes.

Melt the butter and sauté the shallots and wild
mushrooms. Beat together the remaining ingredients.
Arrange the mushroom mixture over the base of the
pastry case. Pour the egg mixture over and bake at
375°F (190°C) gas mark 5 for 35–40 minutes until just
set and golden brown.

Serves 4–6
***

FENNEL & ALMOND RISOTTO

Butter 1 oz (25 g)
Oil 2 tbsp (30 ml)
Whole almonds 4 oz (100 g)
Fennel, sliced 6 oz (175 g)
Onion, sliced 6 oz (175 g)
Short grain or risotto brown rice 8 oz (225 g)
Tomatoes 14 oz can (400 g can)
Shelled peas 4 oz (100 g)
Vegetable stock 1 pt (600 ml)
Lemon, grated rind of ½
Vegetable extract to taste
Salt & pepper to taste

Heat the butter and oil and sauté the whole almonds until golden. Remove from the pan.

Sauté the fennel and onion until transparent, then add the rice and cook, stirring until the rice grains glisten with the fat.

Add the tomatoes, peas and stock and simmer gently for about 45 minutes until the liquid is absorbed and the rice is tender. Stir in the lemon rind, vegetable extract and seasoning to taste. Stir in the almonds.

Serve with a mixed leaf salad.

Serves 4
***

GOATS CHEESE FONDUE

Goat's cheese gives this fondue a wonderfully special flavour. Serve with chunks of wholemeal bread and raw vegetables – cauliflower and celery go well.

Goats cheese, finely crumbled 12 oz (350 g)
Gruyère or Emmenthal, finely grated 4 oz (100 g)
Dry white wine ½ pt (300 ml)
Arrowroot 1 tbsp (15 ml)
Kirsch 2 tbsp (30 ml)
Pepper to taste
Ground nutmeg to taste

Place the cheeses and wine in a saucepan over a very gentle heat (or use a fondue pan) and stir frequently until the cheese has melted.

Mix the arrowroot and kirsch together and stir into the cheese until thickened.

Season to taste with pepper and ground nutmeg.

Serves 4–6

ALIGOTE

A wickedly rich mixture of potato, cream and cheese.
Serve it with a simple salad.

Potatoes 2 lb (900 g)
Soured cream ¼ pt (150 ml)
Milk 2 fl oz (50 ml)
Cheddar cheese, grated 8 oz (225 g)
Salt & pepper to taste

Cut the potatoes into chunks and steam or cook in boiling water for about 20 minutes until tender. Drain and mash.

Place the soured cream, milk and cheese in a saucepan. Mix in the potato and warm gently until the cheese is melted. Season to taste. More milk can be added to give a softer texture.

Variations
Add French mustard to taste.
Add crispy fried onion or garlic to taste.

Serves **4**

LEEK & SESAME SUET PUDDING

A thick leek sauce captured inside a sesame and sage
suet pastry crust.

Butter 2 oz (50 g)
Leeks, thickly sliced 1½ lb (675 g)
Wholemeal flour 2 oz (50 g)
Milk ¾ pt (450 ml)
Parsley, chopped ½ oz (15 g)
Salt & pepper to taste

SUET PASTRY
Vegetable suet 3 oz (75 g) (see p. 6)
Wholemeal self-raising flour 6 oz (175 g)
Sesame seeds 1 oz (25 g)
Dried sage 2 tsp (10 ml)
Water ¼ pt (150 ml)

Melt the butter and sauté the leeks for 10 minutes. Stir
in the flour and cook for 1 minute. Stir in the milk,
parsley and seasoning to taste. Simmer gently, stirring
until thickened. Leave to cool.

For the pastry mix together the suet, flour, sesame
seeds and sage. Season well and mix in the water to
give a soft dough.

Butter a 3 pt (1.8 l) capacity pudding basin. Roll out
three quarters of the pastry and use to line the basin.
Spoon in the sauce, then fold the top of the pastry
inwards.

Roll out the remaining pastry and damp the edges.
Press on top of the leeks to make a lid, sealing the
edges well. Cover with pleated buttered foil or
greaseproof paper and secure well. Steam for 2 hours.

Uncover and serve straight from the pudding basin.

Serves 4–6

SUNFLOWER SAUSAGES

Highly flavoured sausages made from sunflower
seeds and peanuts.

Oil 2 tbsp (30 ml)
Onion, finely chopped 6 oz (175 g)
Sunflower seeds 4 oz (100 g)
Peanuts 4 oz (100 g)
Fresh wholemeal breadcrumbs 4 oz (100 g)
Yeast or vegetable extract 2 tsp (10 ml)
Tomato purée 2 tsp (10 ml)
Mixed dried herbs 2 tsp (10 ml)
Mustard powder ½ tsp (2.5 ml)
Free-range egg, beaten 1
Vegetable stock 2 tbsp (30 ml)
Salt & pepper to taste
Oil for frying

Heat the oil and sauté the onion until golden. Place
the sunflower seeds, peanuts and breadcrumbs in a
food processor with the onion and blend until fairly
smooth. Add the remaining ingredients and blend
again.

Shape the mixture into 8 sausages. Shallow fry until
golden on all sides. Serve with rich brown onion
sauce or tomato sauce (see p. 86 or p. 85).

Serves 4
***

SUNFLOWER POPOVERS

Sunflower sausage mixture (see p. 59) 1 quantity
Oil 8 tsp (40 ml)
Wholemeal flour 4 oz (100 g)
Free-range egg 1
Milk ¼ pt (150 ml)
Water ¼ pt (150 ml)
Salt & pepper to taste

Shape the sunflower sausage mixture into 8 balls.
Place each one in a 4 in (10 cm) individual tin with
1 tsp (5 ml) oil.

Combine the remaining ingredients together to
form a thin batter.

Heat the oven at 425°F (220°C) gas mark 7 and
place the tins in the oven for 5 minutes.

Stir the batter and add a little extra water if
necessary – it should be the consistency of single
cream.

Divide the batter between the tins and return to the
oven as quickly as possible. Bake for about 30 minutes
until golden and crisp.

Serve at once with red wine sauce or rich brown
onion sauce (see p. 89 or p. 86).

Serves 4

VEGETABLE GOULASH

Oil 2 tbsp (30 ml)
Onion, sliced 6 oz (175 g)
Paprika 1 tbsp (15 ml)
Tomatoes, sliced 12 oz (350 g)
Garlic cloves, crushed 2
Ground bayleaf ¼ tsp (1.25 ml)
Tomato juice ¾ pt (450 ml)
Potato, cut into large dice 8 oz (225 g)
White cabbage, cut into large dice 8 oz (225 g)
Aubergines, cut into large dice 6 oz (175 g)
Green pepper, deseeded and sliced 1
Salt & pepper to taste

Heat the oil and sauté the onion and paprika until the onion is soft. Add the tomatoes, garlic, bayleaf, tomato juice and potatoes, and simmer covered for 20 minutes, stirring occasionally.

Add the remaining ingredients and simmer for a further 20 minutes. Season to taste.

Serve with natural yoghourt or soured cream, and freshly cooked rice.

Serves 4
***

SPINACH & TOFU LASAGNE

Use the "no-cook" lasagne sheets for this recipe – then
it's quite quick to make.

Oil 2 tbsp (30 ml)
Garlic cloves, crushed 2
Spinach, chopped 1 lb (450 g)
Tofu, diced 10 oz (300 g)
Soya sauce 1 tbsp (15 ml)
Lemon Juice 1 tbsp (15 ml)
Ground nutmeg, a generous pinch
Wholewheat lasagne 12 sheets
Tomato sauce (see p. 85) 1 quantity
Fresh wholemeal breadcrumbs 1 oz (25 g)
Ground almonds 1 oz (25 g)
Salt & pepper to taste

Heat the oil and sauté the garlic and spinach until it
has just wilted and no liquid remains. Stir in the tofu,
soya sauce, lemon juice and nutmeg and season
generously.

Butter a large ovenproof dish and layer up the
spinach mixture, lasagne sheets and tomato sauce,
finishing with a layer of tomato sauce.

Sprinkle with breadcrumbs and almonds and bake
at 375°F (190°C) gas mark 5 for 30–40 minutes until
bubbling and golden.

Serves 4–6
***

CHEESE & ONION PANCAKES

Butter 2 oz (50 g)
Onion, finely chopped 4 oz (100 g)
Flaked almonds 2 oz (50 g)
Cottage cheese 8 oz (225 g)
Free-range egg, beaten 1
Parmesan cheese, grated 1 oz (25 g)
Thick set, natural yoghourt 4 fl oz (100 ml)
Ground nutmeg, a pinch
Salt & pepper to taste
Wholemeal or buckwheat pancakes (see p. 64) 1 quantity

Melt half the butter and sauté the onion until transparent, add the almonds and continue cooking until golden. Leave to cool.

Combine the onion mixture with the cottage cheese, beaten egg, parmesan cheese, yoghourt and nutmeg. Season to taste.

Spoon a little of the cheese mixture into the centre of each pancake, then fold in the sides to completely encase the filling. Place the "parcels" in a buttered ovenproof dish. Melt the remaining butter and brush the surface of the pancakes. Bake at 400°F (200°C) gas mark 6 for 20–25 minutes until heated through.

Serves 4–6

WHOLEMEAL PANCAKES

Wholemeal flour 8 oz (225 g)
Salt, a pinch
Free-range eggs 2
Milk ¾ pt (450 ml)

Put the flour and salt in a basin. Add the eggs and a little of the milk. Whisk until the mixture is smooth and free of lumps. Gradually add the rest of the milk to make a smooth batter. If necessary add a little more milk if it seems too thick. Allow to stand for 30 minutes.

Pour the batter into a jug. Heat an 8 in (20 cm) pancake pan and grease it well. Pour about 3 tbsp of batter into the pan, swirling it around evenly. Cook the pancake over a medium heat until light golden brown. Turn and cook the other side.

Repeat until the batter is all used up.

Variation
To make buckwheat pancakes use half wholemeal flour and half buckwheat flour.

Makes 8–10 pancakes
***

TRADITIONAL TORTILLA

Cold wedges of tortilla are ideal for packed lunches.

Butter 1 oz (25 g)
Oil 1 tbsp (15 ml)
Potatoes, cut into small dice 8 oz (225 g)
Green pepper, deseeded and diced 1
Onion, diced 4 oz (100 g)
Garlic cloves, sliced 2
Free-range eggs 6
Parsley, chopped 4 tbsp (60 ml)
Salt & pepper to taste

Heat the butter and oil (in an 8–9 in (20–23 cm) frying pan) and sauté the potatoes until golden on all sides. Add the green pepper, onion and garlic and continue cooking until the onion is transparent.

Beat the eggs with the parsley and season generously. Pour the eggs over the vegetables and stir for 1–2 minutes over a medium heat until lightly set.

Reduce the heat, cover and cook for about 15 minutes until completely set. Transfer to a plate. Serve warm or cold in wedges.

Serves 4–6

STILTON, CAULIFLOWER & WALNUT SOUFFLE

A soufflé is easy to make, but timing is vital. It must be served straight from the oven.

Fresh wholemeal breadcrumbs 2 tbsp (30 ml)
Butter 1½ oz (40 g)
Wholemeal flour 1½ oz (40 g)
Milk 8 fl oz (250 ml)
Stilton, crumbled 6 oz (175 g)
Free-range eggs, separated 3
Cauliflower florets, cooked and chopped 8 oz (225 g)
Walnuts, chopped 1 oz (25 g)
Salt & pepper to taste

Butter a 1¾ pt (1 l) soufflé dish and shake the breadcrumbs over the inside to coat evenly. Chill until required.

Melt the butter, stir in the flour and cook for one to two minutes. Add the milk and cook stirring over a medium heat until thickened.

Stir in the stilton and beat in the egg yolks. Fold in the cooked cauliflower and season generously.

Stiffly whisk the egg whites with a pinch of salt and fold into the cheese mixture. Transfer to the prepared dish, sprinkle the top with walnuts and bake at 400°F (200°C) gas mark 6 for about 45 minutes until risen and golden, and just set if lightly shaken. Serve at once.

Serves 4

VEGETABLE & FRUIT COUSCOUS

Couscous 8 oz (225 g)
Oil 2 tbsp (30 ml)
Large onion, chopped 1
Garlic cloves, sliced 2
Ground cinnamon ½ tsp (2.5 ml)
Ground nutmeg ¼ tsp (1.25 ml)
Chilli powder, a generous pinch
Carrot, cut into large dice 8 oz (225 g)
Small okra 6 oz (175 g)
Chick peas, soaked overnight and cooked 4 oz (100 g)
Dried apricots, quartered 2 oz (50 g)
Currants 2 oz (50 g)
Tomatoes, diced 4
Bayleaf 1
Vegetable stock 1 pt (600 ml)
Cashew nuts, toasted 2 oz (50 g)
Salt & pepper to taste

Wash the couscous under cold, running water, then leave to soak in plenty of water whilst preparing the vegetables.

Heat the oil and sauté the onion, garlic and spices. Add the carrot and okra and sauté for a further 2–3 minutes. Add the remaining ingredients. Cover and simmer for 10 minutes.

Place a muslin-lined steamer over the vegetable mixture. Drain the couscous thoroughly and transfer to the steamer. Cover and cook for 15–20 minutes until both the couscous and the vegetables below are tender. Season to taste.

Transfer the couscous to a large serving dish and pile the vegetables in the centre.

Sprinkle with the cashew nuts.

Serves 4

CRANKS DEEP PAN PIZZA

DOUGH
Dried yeast 1 tbsp (15 ml)
Tepid water ¼ pt (150 ml)
Unrefined brown sugar 1 tbsp (15 ml)
Salt ½ tsp (2.5 ml)
Soya flour 2 oz (50 g)
Wholemeal flour 6 oz (175 g)
Oil 2 tbsp (30 ml)

SAUCE
Oil 2 tbsp (30 ml)
Garlic clove, crushed 1
Onion, sliced 8 oz (225 g)
Tomatoes 14 oz can (400 g can)
Tomato purée 1 tbsp (15 ml)
Dried oregano 1 tsp (5 ml)
Dried basil 1 tsp (5 ml)
Bayleaf 1
Salt & pepper to taste

TOPPING
Aubergine 8 oz (225 g)
Oil 2–3 tbsp (30–45 ml)
Red pepper, deseeded and cut into rings 1
Mozzarella cheese, sliced 5 oz (150 g)
Red Leicester or Cheddar cheese, grated 2 oz (50 g)
Fresh marjoram, chopped 1 tbsp (15 ml)

Dough
Mix the yeast with the water and sugar and leave in a warm place to froth.

Combine all the ingredients together and work to a smooth dough. Knead for 5 minutes then place in an oiled basin, cover and leave in a warm place until doubled in size. Meanwhile, make the sauce.

Sauce

Heat the oil and sauté the garlic and onion until transparent. Add the remaining ingredients and cook rapidly, stirring frequently for about 15 minutes until reduced to a thick sauce. Remove the bayleaf and season to taste.

Topping

Cut the aubergine into 8 slices, sprinkle with salt and leave for at least 30 minutes. Rinse and thoroughly dry. Heat the oil and sauté the aubergine slices and the pepper rings until just tender.

Press the dough into an oiled 10 in (25 cm) sandwich tin, making the edge come up the sides of the tin. Spread the sauce over the dough, then top with the aubergine and pepper slices.

Lay the mozzarella on top and sprinkle with the grated cheese and chopped marjoram.

Bake at 425°F (220°C) gas mark 7 for 25–30 minutes until bubbling and golden. Serve warm.

Serves 4–6
***

SPICED VEGETABLES

Takes time to prepare but is quick and easy to cook.

Oil 2 tbsp (30 ml)
Onion, sliced 8 oz (225 g)
Garlic clove, sliced 2
Ground coriander 2 tsp (10 ml)
Ground cumin 1 tsp (5 ml)
Turmeric ½ tsp (2.5 ml)
Ground cardamom ¼ tsp (1.25 ml)
Ground cloves ¼ tsp (1.25 ml)
Curry powder 1 tsp (5 ml)
Root ginger, grated ½ in piece (1 cm piece)
Coriander seeds, crushed ½ tsp (2.5 ml)
Cumin seeds ½ tsp (2.5 ml)
Mustard seeds and Fenugreek ¼ tsp (1.25 ml) each
Black peppercorns, roughly crushed ¼ tsp (1.25 ml)
Tomatoes, chopped 8 oz (225 g)
Tomato purée 1 tbsp (15 ml)
Tomato juice 1 pt (600 ml)
Carrots, sliced 8 oz (225 g)
Potato, diced 8 oz (225 g)
Cauliflower florets 6 oz (175 g)
Courgettes, sliced 6 oz (175 g)
Broccoli florets 4 oz (100 g)
Salt & pepper to taste
Desiccated coconut, toasted and fresh coriander to garnish

Heat the oil and sauté the onion and garlic with the spices until the onion is tender. Add the tomatoes, purée and juice, carrots and potatoes. Simmer for 15 minutes. Add the remaining ingredients. Simmer for a further 10–15 minutes.

Season to taste, garnish and serve with freshly cooked rice.

Serves 4
***

PAELLA – CRANKS STYLE

Baby globe artichokes have a short season and are available in the autumn (see p. 7). Brussels sprouts make a good alternative when artichokes are not available.

Baby globe artichokes 12 oz (350 g)
Saffron strands, a generous pinch
Vegetable stock 1 pt (600 ml)
Oil 3 tbsp (45 ml)
Onions, chopped 12 oz (350 g)
Paprika 2 tsp (10 ml)
Garlic cloves, crushed 3
Brown risotto rice 12 oz (350 g)
Red pepper, deseeded and cut into large dice 1
Green pepper, deseeded and cut into large dice 1
Yellow pepper, deseeded and cut into large dice 1
Fine green beans 4 oz (100 g)
Tomatoes, cut into large dice 4
Black olives, pitted 12
Brazil nuts, toasted 2 oz (50 g)

Steam or cook the baby artichokes in boiling, salted water for 10 minutes or until tender, and keep to one side. Soak the saffron in the vegetable stock until required.

Heat the oil in a large frying pan or paella pan and sauté the onion, paprika and garlic until soft. Add the saffron stock, rice, peppers and green beans. Bring to the boil, reduce the heat and simmer for 20 minutes.

Add the tomatoes and simmer for a further 10 minutes until the rice is tender and all the stock has been absorbed. Add the baby artichokes, olives and brazil nuts and heat gently.

Serves 4–6
***

CHESTNUT MUSHROOM ROULADE

Filling: *Dried chestnuts, soaked overnight 2 oz (50 g)*
Butter 1 oz (25 g)
Onion, finely chopped 2 oz (50 g)
Chestnut mushrooms, finely chopped 4 oz (100 g)
Cream cheese 4 oz (100 g)
Fresh mint, chopped 1 tbsp (15 ml)
Mushroom ketchup 2 tsp (10 ml)
Ground nutmeg, a pinch
Salt & pepper to taste
Soufflé mixture: *Butter 1½ oz (40 g)*
Wholemeal flour 1½ oz (40 g)
Milk 8 fl oz (250 ml)
Free-range eggs, separated 3
Cheddar cheese, grated 4 oz (100 g)

For the filling, drain the chestnuts and cook in fresh water or vegetable stock for about 45 minutes until tender. Drain and finely chop. Melt the butter and sauté the onions and mushrooms. Leave to cool, then add the chestnuts and remaining ingredients. Season with nutmeg, salt and pepper.

Line a Swiss roll tin with baking parchment.

For the soufflé mixture, melt the butter, stir in the flour and cook for 1 minute. Add the milk, stirring all the time until thickened. Remove from the heat and beat in the egg yolks and cheese. Season generously. Stiffly whisk the egg whites and fold into the cheese mixture. Transfer to the prepared tin and level the surface. Bake at 400°F (200°C) gas mark 6 for 15 minutes until risen and just firm to the touch. Unmould onto a clean tea towel, cover with a damp towel. Leave to cool.

Remove the lining paper and spread the filling to the edges. Roll up from a short end. Serve in slices.

Serves 4–6
***

PROTEIN BURGERS

Soya beans, soaked overnight 4 oz (100 g)
Oil 1 tbsp (15 ml)
Onion, finely diced 2 oz (50 g)
Green pepper, deseeded and finely diced ½
Carrot, finely grated 8 oz (225 g)
Soya bean sprouts 2 oz (50 g)
Tofu 4 oz (100 g)
Salt & pepper to taste
Soya sauce to taste
Oil for frying

COATING
Wheatgerm 1 oz (25 g)
Sesame seeds ½ oz (15 g)

Drain the beans, then bring to the boil in fresh water. Boil for 10 minutes, reduce the heat and simmer for 2–3 hours until tender, adding extra water as necessary. Drain and blend in a liquidizer or food processor until fairly smooth.

Heat the oil and sauté the onion and green pepper. Squeeze excess liquid from the grated carrot by drying on a tea towel.

Combine the puréed soya beans, onion mixture, carrot, soya bean sprouts and tofu. Season generously with soya sauce, salt and pepper and shape into 8 burgers.

Mix the wheatgerm and sesame seeds and evenly coat the burgers. Fry in hot, shallow oil until golden on both sides.

Serves 4: Makes 8
***

FRESH DILL & PINE NUT RAVIOLI

There is nothing quite like homemade ravioli!

DOUGH
Wholemeal flour 8 oz (225 g)
Salt 1 tsp (5 ml)
Free-range eggs, beaten 2
Olive oil 2 tsp (10 ml)
Water 2 tbsp (30 ml)

FILLING
Butter 1 oz (25 g)
Shallots, finely chopped 4 oz (100 g)
Pine kernels 2 oz (50 g)
Fresh dill, chopped 4 tbsp (60 ml)
Cream or curd cheese 8 oz (225 g)
Salt & pepper to taste
Semolina for rolling the dough
Beaten egg to seal

Combine all the ingredients for the dough until smooth. Cover and leave to rest.

Melt the butter and sauté the shallots and pine kernels until lightly golden. Leave to cool, then combine with the remaining ingredients. Season to taste.

Divide the dough into 4 equal portions. Sprinkle the work surface with a little semolina and roll out 2 pieces of the dough to about 11 in (28 cm) squares. Using half the filling, position 16 small mounds, evenly spaced on one piece of the dough.

Brush between the gaps with the beaten egg and cover with the other piece of dough. Press down well to seal, then cut into squares with a ravioli cutter or sharp knife.

Repeat with the remaining dough and filling. Bring a large saucepan of salted water to the boil. Add a drop of oil. Cook the ravioli for about 15 minutes until tender. Drain well.

Serve with plenty of melted butter or butter sauce (see p. 90).

Serves 4
***

BEETROOT, APPLE & POTATO RAGOUT

Butter 1 oz (25 g)
Oil 1 tbsp (15 ml)
Onion, thickly sliced 12 oz (350 g)
Raw beetroot, cut into large dice 1½ lb (675 g)
Vegetable stock ½ pt (300 ml)
Potatoes, cut into large dice 1 lb (450 g)
Dessert apples, cored and cut into eighths 1 lb (450 g)
Apple concentrate 2 tbsp (30 ml)
Cider or wine vinegar 2 tbsp (30 ml)
Salt & pepper to taste

Heat the butter and oil and sauté the onion until transparent. Add the beetroot and stock and bring to the boil. Cover and simmer for 40 minutes.

Add the potatoes and cook for a further 20 minutes. Add the remaining ingredients and simmer for 10 minutes. Season to taste.

Serve with natural yoghourt or soured cream.

Serves 4–6

GREEN & WHITE TERRINE

An elegant dish for a dinner party.

Broccoli 1 lb (450 g)
Cauliflower 1 lb (450 g)
Free-range eggs 2
Double cream 2 tbsp (30 ml)
Spring onions, chopped 2 tbsp (30 ml)
Lemon juice 1 tbsp (15 ml)
Ground mace ¼ tsp (1.25 ml)
Salt & pepper to taste
Whole almonds, toasted to garnish
Parsley sprigs to garnish

Steam the broccoli and cauliflower separately for about 15 minutes until tender. Drain well. Blend the cauliflower in a liquidizer or food processor with 1 egg, 1 tbsp (15 ml) cream and mace; season generously with salt and pepper.

Blend the broccoli with 1 egg, 1 tbsp (15 ml) cream, spring onions and lemon juice. Season generously with salt and pepper.

Butter a 2 lb (900 g) loaf tin and line the base. Spoon in one mixture and level the surface. Carefully spoon in the other mixture and level the surface. Cover and cook in the oven, in a bain marie, at 400°F (200°C) gas mark 6 for about 50 minutes until just firm.

Unmould and garnish with whole almonds and parsley sprigs. Serve with almond sauce (see p. 90).

Serves 6

SPINACH, LENTIL & TOFU ROULADE

Soufflé mixture: *Spinach 4 oz (100 g)*
Milk 8 fl oz (250 ml)
Butter 1½ oz (40 g)
Wholemeal flour 1½ oz (40 g)
Free-range eggs 3
Cheddar cheese, grated 4 oz (100 g)
Filling: *Butter 1 oz (25 g)*
Onion, finely chopped 4 oz (100 g)
Red lentils 2 oz (50 g)
Vegetable stock ½ pt (300 ml)
Smoked tofu, finely diced 3 oz (75 g)
Parsley, chopped 1 tbsp (15 ml)
Lemon juice 1 tsp (5 ml)
Salt & pepper to taste

Line a Swiss roll tin with baking parchment. Purée the spinach and milk in a liquidizer. Melt the butter, stir in the flour and cook for 1 minute. Add the milk, stirring all the time until thickened. Remove from the heat and beat in the egg yolks and cheese. Season generously.

Stiffly whisk the egg whites and fold into the cheese mixture. Transfer to the prepared tin and level the surface. Bake at 400°F (200°C) gas mark 6 for 15 minutes until risen and just firm to the touch.

To make the filling, melt the butter and sauté the onion. Add the lentils and stock and cook until tender and no liquid remains. Stir in remaining ingredients and season to taste.

Unmould the roulade onto a clean tea towel. Remove the lining paper and spread the filling to the edges. Roll up from a short end. Serve in slices.

Serves 4–6
***

BRAZILIAN BLACK BEAN STEW

Black kidney beans, soaked overnight 8 oz (225 g)
Oranges 2
Butter 1 oz (25 g)
Oil 1 tbsp (15 ml)
Onion, chopped 8 oz (225 g)
Celery, sliced 8 oz (225 g)
Fresh chilli, chopped 1
Garlic cloves, sliced 2
Tomatoes 8 oz (225 g)
Vegetable extract 2 tsp (10 ml)
Unrefined brown sugar 1 tbsp (15 ml)
Tomato purée 1 tbsp (15 ml)
Bayleaf 1
Dried rosemary 1 tsp (5 ml)
Salt & pepper to taste

Drain the beans, then bring them to the boil in fresh water. Boil for 15 minutes, then reduce the heat and simmer for 45 minutes. Drain, reserving ¾ pt (450 ml) cooking liquid.

Pare the rind from the oranges. Discard the white pith and roughly chop the fruit.

Heat the butter and oil and sauté the onion, celery, chilli and garlic until the onion is transparent. Add the beans with their cooking liquid, the orange peel and remaining ingredients. Bring to the boil, reduce the heat, cover and simmer for 30 minutes. Add the orange pieces. Season to taste and cook for a further 10–15 minutes.

Serves 4–6
***

VEGETABLE STIR FRY

Oil 3 tbsp (45 ml)
Garlic cloves, sliced 3
Root ginger, grated 1 in (2.5 cm) piece
Carrot, thinly sliced 6 oz (175 g)
Baby sweetcorn 6 oz (175 g)
Large red pepper, deseeded and diced 1
Leek, thinly sliced 6 oz (175 g)
Beansprouts 6 oz (175 g)
Mangetout 6 oz (175 g)
Chinese leaves, shredded 6 oz (175 g)
Dry sherry 2 tbsp (30 ml)
Soya sauce 2 tbsp (30 ml)
Vegetable stock ¼ pt (150 ml)
Arrowroot 2 tsp(10 ml)

Heat the oil in a large frying pan or wok. Add the garlic, ginger, carrots and sweetcorn and cook, stirring all the time over a high heat for 2 minutes.

Add the red pepper and leek and stir fry for 1–2 minutes. Add the remaining vegetables and stir fry for a further 1 minute.

Combine the sherry, soya sauce, vegetable stock and arrowroot, pour over the vegetables and bring to the boil, stirring until thickened.

Serve at once.

Serves 4–6

RAISED VEGETABLE & NUT PIE

A rather involved recipe, but the end result is
spectacular. Make at least one day before required.

FILLING I
Butter ½ oz (15 g)
Onion, finely chopped 4 oz (100 g)
Garlic clove, crushed 1
Celery sticks, finely chopped 2
Ground cumin 1 tsp (5 ml)
Paprika 1 tsp (5 ml)
Dried basil 1 tsp (5 ml)
Vegetable stock ¼ pt (150 ml)
Red wine ¼ pt (150 ml)
Cooked chestnuts, finely chopped 4 oz (100 g)
Brazil nuts, finely chopped 4 oz (100 g)
Pecan nuts, finely chopped 4 oz (100 g)
Wholemeal breadcrumbs 2 oz (50 g)
Parsley, chopped 4 tbsp (60 ml)
Soya sauce 1 tbsp (15 ml)
Brandy 1 tbsp (15 ml)
Free-range eggs, beaten 2
Salt & pepper to taste

FILLING II
Carrot, roughly chopped 1 lb (450 g)
Double cream 1 tbsp (15 ml)
Coconut milk powder 1 tbsp (15 ml)
Free-range egg, beaten 1

Hot water crust pastry (see p. 8) 1 quantity
Beaten egg to glaze 1

To make Filling I, melt the butter and sauté the onion,
garlic, celery, cumin, paprika and basil until the onion
is soft. Add the vegetable stock and wine, bring to the
boil. Remove from the heat and add the remaining
ingredients. Season generously and leave to cool.

To make Filling II, steam the carrots for 15–20 minutes until tender, then blend in a liquidizer or food processor with the remaining ingredients. Season generously. Leave to cool.

Roll out about two thirds of the pastry and use to line a 7 in (18 cm) round loose-bottomed, deep-sided cake tin. Spoon in the first filling and level the surface. Top with the carrot filling and level the surface.

Roll out the remaining pastry and use to top the pie, sealing the edges well with beaten egg. Stamp out a 1 in (2.5 cm) circle of pastry from the centre. Trim and crimp the edge of the pastry and use the trimmings to make pastry "leaves" and a "tassel". To make the tassel, cut a piece of pastry 4 in (10 cm) long and 1 in (2.5 cm) wide. Cut frequent slits along the length of the pastry, then roll up from the short end and ease out to form a tassel. Brush the pie with beaten egg and position the leaves. Brush the tassel with egg and place on a baking sheet. Bake the pie in the oven at 400°F (200°C) gas mark 6 for 1¼–1½ hours until golden brown. Cook the tassel for about 20 minutes until golden brown.

Leave the pie until completely cold before unmoulding. Position the tassel.

If wished, make up ¼ pt (150 ml) of agar flakes with vegetable stock according to packet directions and pour into the pie. Leave to set then replace the tassel.

Serves 8–10
***

TOMATO, AVOCADO & MOZZARELLA BAKE

Simple to make – exceedingly good to eat!

Ripe avocados 2
Mediterranean tomatoes, sliced 2
Mozzarella cheese, sliced 8 oz (225 g)
Butter sauce (see p. 90) 1 quantity
Fresh basil leaves, shredded 18

Halve, peel and remove the stones from the avocados. Cut into thick slices.

Arrange the avocado, tomato and mozzarella slices in four individual ovenproof dishes.

Pour some of the butter sauce over each portion and sprinkle with basil.

Bake at 400°F (200°C) gas mark 6 for about 20 minutes until bubbling.

Serves 4

MEXICAN MUSHROOM FLATS

Mushroom flats or caps 1 lb (450 g)
Butter 1 oz (25 g)
Onion, chopped 4 oz (100 g)
Garlic cloves, crushed 2
Spinach, shredded 8 oz (225 g)
Tofu, chopped 6oz (175 g)
Salt & pepper to taste

Wipe the mushrooms, remove the stalks and roughly chop them.

Melt the butter and sauté the onion, garlic and mushroom stalks. Add the spinach and cook quickly until it just wilts and no liquid remains. Remove from the heat. Stir in the tofu and season generously.

Place the mushroom flats in a large buttered ovenproof dish. Divide the filling between the mushrooms, cover and bake at 400°F (200°C) gas mark 6 for 20 minutes.

Serve with spicy tomato sauce (see p. 91).

Serves 4

KOHLRABI & COURGETTE PIE

Kohlrabi 1¼ lb (550 g)
Courgettes 1 lb (450 g)
Cream sauce (see p. 93) 1 quantity
Gruyère cheese, grated 4 oz (100 g)
Salt & pepper to taste
Wholemeal pastry, made using wholemeal flour
(see chart p. 8) 7 oz (200 g)
Free-range egg, beaten 1

Cut the vegetables into batons and steam separately. The kohlrabi will need 15–20 minutes, the courgettes about 5 minutes.

Combine the vegetables with the cream sauce and cheese. Season to taste.

Transfer the mixture to a 2½ pt (1.5 l) pie dish and top with the shortcrust pastry. Brush with beaten egg and bake at 400°F (200°C) gas mark 6 for about 30 minutes until golden brown.

Serves 4
***

CURRY SAUCE

Oil 2 fl oz (50 ml)
Garlic cloves, crushed 2
Onion, finely sliced 12 oz (350 g)
Curry powder 1½ tsp (7.5 ml)
Ground ginger ½ tsp (2.5 ml)
Ground coriander 2 tsp (10 ml)
Ground cumin 1 tsp (5 ml)
Turmeric ½ tsp (2.5 ml)
Ground cloves ¼ tsp (1.25 ml)
Garam masala ½ tsp (2.5 ml)
Chilli powder (optional) a pinch
Tomato juice 1 pt (600 ml)
Salt to taste

Heat the oil and sauté the garlic and onion with the spices until soft. Add the tomato juice, cover and simmer gently for 25–30 minutes, stirring occasionally.

Season to taste with salt.

Makes about 1¼ pt (750 ml).
***

SPINACH SAUCE

Butter 1 oz (25 g)
Onion, chopped 3 oz (75 g)
Garlic clove, chopped 1
Spinach 12 oz (350 g)
Soya sauce 1 tbsp (15 ml)
Lemon juice 1 tbsp (15 ml)
Vegetable concentrate ½ tsp (2.5 ml)
Vegetable stock or water ¼ pt (150 ml)
Single cream ¼ pt (150 ml)
Ground nutmeg, a generous pinch
Salt & pepper to taste

Melt the butter and sauté the onion and garlic until transparent. Add the spinach a little at a time until it wilts. Add the soya sauce, lemon juice, vegetable concentrate and stock.

Cover and simmer for 15 minutes. Stir in the remaining ingredients, allow to cool, then blend in a liquidizer or food processor until smooth.

Season to taste.

Makes about 1 pt (600 ml).
***

FRESH TOMATO SAUCE

Oil 2 tbsp (30 ml)
Onion, chopped 4 oz (100 g)
Garlic clove, crushed 1
Dried oregano 1 tsp (5 ml)
Dried basil 1 tsp (5 ml)
Bayleaf 1
Wholemeal flour 1 oz (25 g)
Tomato juice ½ pt (300 ml)
Tomato purée 1 tbsp (15 ml)
Tomatoes, chopped 1 lb (450 g)
Red wine or sherry 2 tbsp (30 ml)
Soya sauce 1 tbsp (15 ml)
Parsley, chopped 1 tbsp (15 ml)
Salt & pepper to taste

Heat the oil and sauté the onion and garlic until transparent. Add the herbs and flour and cook, stirring for 1 minute.

Add the remaining ingredients except the parsley. Bring to the boil, reduce heat, cover and simmer for 20 minutes. Remove the bayleaf, add the parsley and season to taste.

Makes about 1½ pt (900 ml).
***

RICH BROWN ONION SAUCE

Oil 3 tbsp (45 ml)
Medium onions, sliced 2
Garlic cloves, crushed 2
Wholemeal flour 2 tbsp (30 ml)
Vegetable extract ½ tsp (2.5 ml)
Yeast extract ½ tsp (2.5 ml)
Soya sauce 2 tbsp (30 ml)
Tomato purée 1 tbsp (15 ml)
Red wine ¼ pt (150 ml)
Vegetable stock ½ pt (300 ml)
Parsley, chopped 2 tbsp (30 ml)
Salt & pepper to taste

Heat the oil and sauté the onion and garlic until golden. Stir in the flour and cook for 1 minute. Add the remaining ingredients except the parsley.

Bring to the boil, reduce the heat and simmer for 20 minutes. Add the parsley and season to taste.

Makes about 1 pt (600 ml).
***

CHEESE SAUCE

Oil 2 tbsp (30 ml)
Onion, sliced 8 oz (225 g)
Ground bayleaf ½ tsp (2.5 ml)
Fresh thyme 2 tsp (10 ml)
Wholemeal flour 2 oz (50 g)
Prepared English mustard 2 tsp (10 ml)
Vegetable extract 1 tsp (5 ml)
Milk 1 pt (600 ml)
Cheddar cheese, grated 6 oz (175 g)

Ground coriander 1 tsp (5 ml)
Ground mace ½ tsp (2.5 ml)
Cayenne, a pinch
Salt & pepper to taste

Heat the oil and sauté the onion, with the ground bayleaf and thyme, until soft. Add the flour, mustard and vegetable extract and cook, stirring, for 1–2 minutes.

Stir in the milk and bring to the boil stirring constantly. Add the remaining ingredients and stir gently until the cheese has melted. Season to taste.

Makes about 1½ pt (900 ml).
***

PROVENÇALE SAUCE

Oil 2 tbsp (30 ml)
Onion, sliced 6 oz (175 g)
Ground bayleaf ½ tsp (2.5 ml)
Dried oregano 1 tsp (5ml)
Dried basil 1 tsp (5 ml)
Garlic cloves, sliced 2
Tomatoes, sliced 12 oz (350 g)
Tomato juice ½ pt (300 ml)
Tomato purée 2 tbsp (30 ml)
Unrefined brown sugar 2 tsp (10 ml)
Parsley, chopped 4 tbsp (60 ml)
Paprika 1 tsp (5 ml)
Olives, pitted and chopped 4 oz (100 g)
Salt & pepper to taste

Heat the oil and sauté the onion with the herbs and garlic. Add the tomatoes, tomato juice, tomato purée and sugar. Simmer gently for 30 minutes.

Add the remaining ingredients and season to taste.

Makes about 1 pt (600 ml).
***

LEMON SAUCE

Butter 1 oz (25 g)
Onion, chopped 4 oz (100 g)
Carrot, chopped 4 oz (100 g)
Thin skinned lemon, chopped 1
Vegetable stock 1¼ pt (750 ml)
Single cream ¼ pt (150 ml)
Unrefined brown sugar 1 tbsp (15 ml)
Salt & pepper to taste

Melt the butter and sauté the onion and carrot until the onion is transparent. Add the lemon and stock. Cover and simmer for 30 minutes.

Blend in a liquidizer or food processor until smooth. Stir in the cream and sugar and season to taste. Reheat gently.

Makes about 1¾ pt (1 l).
***

WHITE WINE SAUCE

Butter 1 oz (25 g)
Wholemeal flour 2 tbsp (30 ml)
Milk ½ pt (300 ml)
Dry white wine ¼ pt (150 ml)
Bayleaf 1
Ground nutmeg, a large pinch
Salt & pepper to taste

Melt the butter, add the flour. Mix well. Cook for 1 minute, stirring all the time. Stir in the milk, then the wine. Add the bayleaf and nutmeg. Simmer gently for 5 minutes, stirring occasionally. Season to taste and remove the bayleaf.

Variations
French Onion Sauce
Sauté 4 oz (100 g) chopped onion in 1 oz (25 g)
butter until golden and add to the white wine sauce;
purée in a liquidizer if wished.

Mushroom Sauce
Sauté 4 oz (100 g) chopped mushrooms in 1 oz (25 g)
butter and add to the white wine sauce.

Lemon & Herb Sauce
Add 3 tbsp (45 ml) chopped fresh herbs (parsley,
mint, chives, tarragon), 1 tsp (5 ml) freshly-grated
lemon rind and lemon juice to taste, to the prepared
sauce.

Makes about ⅔ pt (400 ml).
***

RED WINE SAUCE

Butter 1 oz (25 g)
Medium sized onion, finely chopped 1
Wholemeal flour 2 tbsp (30 ml)
Ripe tomatoes, chopped 3
Dry red wine ½ pt (300 ml)
Vegetable stock ¼ pt (150 ml)
Vegetable extract or yeast extract to taste
Salt & pepper to taste
Parsley, chopped 2 tbsp (30 ml)

Melt the butter and sauté the onion until well
browned. Stir in the flour and cook for 1 minute. Add
the tomatoes, wine and stock; cover and simmer for
20 minutes, then add the vegetable extract and salt
and pepper to taste. Stir in the chopped parsley before
serving. For a thicker consistency, simmer for a little
while uncovered to reduce the sauce.

Makes about 1 pt (600 ml).
***

ALMOND SAUCE

Butter 1 oz (25 g)
Shallots, finely chopped 2 oz (50 g)
Ground almonds 3 oz (75 g)
Vegetable stock ¾ pt (450 ml)
Lemon juice 1 tsp (5 ml)
Arrowroot 1 tsp (5 ml)
Salt & pepper to taste

Melt the butter and sauté the shallots until golden. Dry fry the ground almonds in a heavy based pan, stirring all the time until golden, then add to the shallots, with the vegetable stock.

Cover and simmer for 15–20 minutes. Add the lemon juice, mix the arrowroot with a little water and stir into the sauce. Cook until thickened and season to taste.

Makes about ¾ pt (450 ml).
***

BUTTER SAUCE

Butter 2 oz (50 g)
Wholemeal flour 1½ tbsp (22.5 ml)
Vegetable stock ½ pt (300 ml)
Lemon juice 1 tsp (5 ml)
Salt & pepper to taste

Melt about one third of the butter in a saucepan. Stir in the flour. Bring the stock to the boil and add to the butter mixture, stirring until lightly thickened.

Remove from the heat and whisk in the remaining butter. Season to taste with lemon juice, salt and pepper.

Makes about ½ pt (300 ml).
***

SPICY TOMATO SAUCE

Butter 1 oz (25 g)
Onion, chopped 1
Garlic clove, crushed 1
Dried chillies, crumbled 1–2
Tomatoes, chopped 12 oz (350 g)
Vegetable stock ½ pt (300 ml)
Tomato purée 1 tbsp (15 ml)
Salt & pepper to taste

Melt the butter and sauté the onion, garlic and chillies until the onion is transparent. Add the remaining ingredients and bring to the boil. Reduce the heat and simmer for 15 minutes.

Blend in a liquidizer or food processor. Season to taste.

Makes about 1 pt (600 ml).
***

SAVOURY BROWN SAUCE

Butter 2 oz (50 g)
Large onion, finely chopped 1
Wholemeal flour 2 oz (50 g)
Vegetable stock 1 pt (600 ml)
Yeast extract 1 tbsp (15 ml)
Pepper to taste

Melt the butter and fry the onion until golden brown. Stir in the flour and cook for 2 minutes, stirring occasionally.

Pour in stock and yeast extract, stirring. Bring to the boil, reduce heat, cover and simmer for 10 minutes.

Season to taste.

Blend in a liquidizer or food processor if wished.

Makes about 1 pt (600 ml).
***

BASIC "WHITE" SAUCE

Butter 2 oz (50 g)
Wholemeal flour 2 oz (50 g)
Milk 1 pt (600 ml)
Salt & pepper to taste

Melt the butter in a saucepan and stir in the flour;
cook for 1–2 minutes, stirring occasionally. Slowly stir
in the milk until it is evenly blended. Bring to the boil,
reduce the heat and simmer for 2–3 minutes. Season
to taste.

Variations
Cheese
Add ½ tsp (2.5 ml) mustard powder with the flour.
Stir in 4 oz (100 g) grated Cheddar cheese at the end
of cooking.

Parsley
Add 6 tbsp (90 ml) chopped parsley after the milk.

Makes about 1 pt (600 ml).
***

CREAM SAUCE

Shallots, finely chopped 1 oz (25 g)
Peppercorns, crushed 1 tsp (5 ml)
Dry white wine ¼ pt (150 ml)
Vegetable stock ¾ pt (450 ml)
Double cream ½ pt (300 ml)
Arrowroot 1 tsp (5 ml)
Salt to taste

Place the shallots, peppercorns and wine in a saucepan and boil rapidly until reduced by half. Add the stock and reduce again by half.

Add the cream and arrowroot and whisk over gentle heat until thickened.

Season with salt.

Makes about ¾ pt (450 ml).
***

INDEX

SAVOURIES

SAUCES

**Recipes which are suitable for
freezing are marked by asterisks
*****